ORPHAN TEX'

ORPHAN TEXTS

Victorian orphans, culture and empire

Laura Peters

MANCHESTER UNIVERSITY PRESS
Manchester and New York

distributed exclusively in the USA by St. Martin's Press

Published by Manchester University Press
Oxford Road, Manchester M13 9NR, UK
and Room 400, 175 Fifth Avenue, New York, NY 10010, USA
www.manchesteruniversitypress.co.uk

Distributed in the United States exclusively by
Palgrave Macmillan, 175 Fifth Avenue,
New York, NY 10010, USA

Distributed in Canada exclusively by
UBC Press, University of British Columbia, 2029 West Mall,
Vancouver, BC, Canada V6T 1Z2

British Library Cataloguing-in-Publication Data is available

Library of Congress Cataloging-in-Publication Data is available

ISBN 978 0 7190 9016 5 paperback

First published by Manchester University Press in hardback 2000

This paperback edition first published 2013

The publisher has no responsibility for the persistence or accuracy of URLs for any external or third-party internet websites referred to in this book, and does not guarantee that any content on such websites is, or will remain, accurate or appropriate.

Printed by Lightning Source

Contents

TO MY PARENTS,

WALTER AND NANCY

Acknowledgements

Without the support of many different people this book could never have been written and these brief acknowledgements can only begin to express my gratitude. To Professor Malcolm Andrews, who supervised the PhD thesis that, in some ways, forms the basis of this book, I owe an enormous debt of gratitude for both his work then and his continued support. I am very grateful to Dr Shaun Richards for his support and the timetable alleviation it brought with it; I am also grateful to my colleagues in English who agreed the sabbatical that enabled me to work on this book. I am immensely grateful to David Alderson who acted as reader for this book. His thoroughness and supportive comments certainly improved the book – any remaining shortcomings are my own responsibility.

I must thank my family – my parents, Walter and Nancy, and my sisters, Shelley and Catherine. Their support throughout my life has enabled me to achieve what I have. During the writing of this book my first and much loved son Adam was born. What he has thought of his mother working away on the computer, I am not sure, but he was eager to make his own contributions. The special contribution he has made to my life has made the writing of certain sections especially poignant. Finally, and most importantly, I owe everything to my husband, Azzedine. He has supported me and empowered me. He has challenged me to realise the potential of this book and has been long suffering through the moments of torment that the writing of the book has produced.

Chapter 3, Popular orphan adventure narratives, was published as 'Perilous Adventures: Dickens and popular orphan adventures narratives' in *The Dickensian* 94: 3 (Winter 1998): 172–83. Many thanks for the editor's permission to reprint this.

1

Introduction

ONE CAN hardly open a novel by Dickens, the Brontë sisters, or George Eliot without stumbling over at least one orphan. The orphan is not restricted to these writers but can also be found in plenitude in works by Anthony Trollope, William Makepeace Thackeray, Wilkie Collins, Rudyard Kipling, Oscar Wilde, the poems of Elizabeth Barrett Browning, and *Goblin Market* by Christina Rossetti. The orphan figure was also a recurrent figure in popular culture evident in plays such as *The Factory Lad*, and melodramas such as *Black-Eyed Susan*. The question is then: how can one explain the prevalence of this figure in Victorian culture? What this book argues is that the prevalence of the orphan figure can be explained by the central role which the family played at the time. Although one would expect that orphans needed a family, in short, the reality was that the family needed orphans. The family and all it came to represent – legitimacy, race and national belonging – was in crisis: it was at best an unsustainable ideal. In order to reaffirm itself the family needed a scapegoat. It found one in the orphan figure.

Before I go any further I would like to establish what was understood by the term orphan. On one hand an orphan was one who was without parents. But, in Victorian culture the term also referred to one who was deprived of only one parent. Even more significantly, an orphan was also one who was 'bereft of protection, advantages, benefits, or happiness, previously enjoyed' (*OED*). In other words, the orphan was vulnerable, disadvantaged, miserable. In the City of London the Lord Mayor and Aldermen had custody of orphans of deceased freemen; the state's responsibility to the orphan was through the Board of Guardians of the parish. To what extent the *OED* captures the way Victorians conceived of the orphan remains to be seen, but this book will argue that Victorian culture perceived the orphan as a scapegoat – a promise and a threat, a poison and a cure. As such, the orphan, as one who embodied the loss of the family, came to represent a dangerous threat; the family reaffirmed itself through the expulsion of this threatening difference. The vulnerable and miserable condition of the orphan, as one without rights, enabled it to be conceived of and treated as such by the very structure responsible for its care.

Although there has been immense critical attention on the issues of family and childhood in Victorian culture, there is a dearth of criticism on the orphan. Why this is so, given the prevalence of this figure, is somewhat of a mystery. Although there is a growing interest in issues of genealogy and ancestry, as evidenced by two recent books, Tess O'Toole's *Genealogy and Fiction in Hardy* and Sophie Gilmartin's *Ancestry and Narrative in Nineteenth-Century British Literature*, the problem that the orphan poses for genealogy and ancestry have yet to be addressed. This book seeks to introduce the issue of the orphan into these debates and to go some way to redress the lack of critical analysis of the orphan in Victorian culture. I have chosen to read certain canonical texts alongside lesser known works from popular culture in order to establish the context in which discourses of orphanhood operated.

In the early pages of *Daniel Deronda* – a novel which deals with the illusory nature of home and family origins – George Eliot's narrator offers a meditation on the importance of home and rootedness.

> A human life, I think, should be well rooted in some spot of a native land, where it may get the love of tender kinship for the face of the earth, for the labours men go forth to, for the sounds and accents that haunt it, for whatever will give that early home a familiar unmistakable difference amidst the future widening of knowledge: a spot where the definiteness of early memories may be inwrought with affection, and kindly acquaintance with all neighbours, even

to the dogs and donkeys, may spread not by sentimental effort and reflection, but as a sweet habit of the blood. At five years old, mortals are not prepared to be citizens of the world, to be stimulated by abstract nouns, to soar above preference into impartiality; and that prejudice in favour of milk with which we blindly begin, is a type of the way body and soul must get nourished at least for a time. The best introduction to astronomy is to think of the nightly heavens as a little lot of stars belonging to one's own homestead. (Eliot, 1984: 50)

In stressing the importance of family, home and blood relations, this passage offers a window on to a number of discourses on the importance of the family in circulation during the Victorian era. Firstly, the passage articulates a structure of feeling regarding Victorian attitudes towards family, home and place – the latter term being used in literal, class and metonymic senses. The central importance of middle-class notions of the family and home rest in their functioning as a site of morality, snug domesticity, a haven from the 'amoral world of market' (Davidoff and Hall, 1987: 74), and a beacon welcoming those back from foreign travels and the work of empire. This has been a dominant mode of interpretation, epitomised by Walter Houghton's *The Victorian Frame of Mind, 1830–1870* (Houghton, 1957). To an extent, considering how certain Victorians wrote about their own perceptions, this does not appear misplaced. Ruskin's famous 'Of Queen's Gardens' lecture enshrines this notion of the domestic ideal: 'This is the true nature of home – it is the place of Peace; the shelter, not only from all injury, but from all terror, doubt, and division … it is a sacred place, a vestal temple, a temple of the hearth watched over by Household Gods' (Ruskin, 1902–12: 122). The central shrine in this sacred temple of domesticity is the figure of Woman – a stereotypical construction known as the angel in the house (Auerbach, 1985). Significantly then, Eliot's passage stresses that it is mother's milk (in the form of family and kinship) which nourishes soul and body. It was a widely held view at the time that: 'All the resources of art cannot supply the absence of maternal care, and the influence of that home education which, according to the order of nature, can only flow from a parent's love' (Parliamentary Papers (PP), 1852, XXXIX: 71).[1]

But one should not overlook that this domestic bliss was not only a middle class construction but was the property of the middle classes; in this scheme of things the working classes and the very poor had no right to this. Of pauper children, E.C. Tufnell, in his 1851 Report for the Committee on Education has this to say: 'I do not know of one [pauper child] who, if he has had parents, has been in any way advantaged by them, or rather, who has not at times had to resist the evil example and vicious enticement which they have been too ready to place before him' (PP, 1852, XXXIX: 71). However, such a view was contested by the contemporary working classes and poor themselves and by twentieth-century critics such as Louis James, Martha Vicinus, and others whose work demonstrates the importance of the family and home in working-class and poor cultures (James, 1974, 1978; Vicinus, 1974). James argues that however loosely defined the 'domestic story lies at the heart of almost all penny-issue fiction published during the 1840s' (James, 1974: 14).

In addition, there is an emergent line of argument in twentieth-century criticism that argues that 'this idealization is less than half the picture' (Edmond, 1988: 7); indeed it may have been only half the picture during the Victorian age as well. In 1849 James Froude was writing of a particular kind of homesickness: that of the 'exiled' emigrant in the colonies. 'God has given us each our own Paradise, our own childhood over which the old glories linger – to which our own hearts cling, as all we have ever known of Heaven upon earth. And there, as all earth's weary wayfarers turn back ... in thought, at least, to that old time of peace – that village church – that child-faith – which, once lost, is never gained again' (Froude, 1904: 116). Here then such a notion of home is constructed through a Romantic notion of childhood as before time, out of history. The longing for such a home is then melancholic, in Freud's terms: a process of objectification which keeps what can never be recovered permanently alive through a process of continual mourning and desire (Freud, 1987). Eliot's narrator articulates such a melancholic conception of home and family in an assertion of the familial ideal which refuses to acknowledge that this ideal was increasingly under threat, if not entirely destroyed, by the impact of the rise of capitalism: 'The bourgeoisie has torn away from the family its sentimental veil, and turned the family relation into a pure money relation' (Marx and Engels, 1967: 82). In addition, although espoused as a middle-class ideal, the writing from the middle classes is predominately about failed families, unorthodox families and domestic violence. One need only to look at the work of Charles Dickens, the Brontë sisters, or even George Eliot, to recognise this; it can be identified as melancholic; the keeping alive of an ideal through desiring it in the midst of its loss.

However, when under threat, the proponents of such an ideal are driven to drastic actions. In this case, the domestic ideal was used both as a tool to colonise the poor (Foucault, 1979: 121–2) and as an export to the colonies. There is an impulse, which Graham Dawson identifies, 'to extend the boundaries of "home" [in imperial endeavours] and [to] transform more of the wilderness, through enlightened cultivation, into a garden' (Dawson, 1994: 65). The domestic idyll then becomes a 'rose-covered cottage in a garden where Womanhood waited and from which Man ventured abroad – to work, to war and to the Empire' (Davidoff and Hall, 1987: 28). Such colonial overtones and romantic idealisation can be seen to characterise the opening quotation. The reference to a native land which engenders kinship both with the environment and with the neighbours constructs a notion of an indigenous community bonded through blood relations; a community unified by the 'sounds and accents' of a shared language. Above all the blood relations and shared language give this home – in the sense of the wider community – an unmistakable difference. It is the myth of an essentialised origin to which the memory will return and which will command 'affection' and, crucially, loyalty. However, implicit in this are a number of disturbing assumptions: the reference to blood relations especially in conjunction with notions of native community constructs a racial grouping; the emphasis on indigeneity distinguishes between the 'natives' and the immigrants; the emphasis on rootedness differentiates this community from travelling and diasporic peoples. It is not difficult to recognise here, as the home extends to the community and ultimately to the state, early conceptions of national identity and nationalism: Edward Said argues persuasively that the book's 'main subject is Zionism' (Said, 1979: 18). The book's subject is about Zionism, but it is also *de facto* about the construction/consolidation of an English national identity. Finally, there is the curious, but revealing passage, about the nightly heavens belonging to one's own homestead – a desire that can be read as colonial in nature in its need to construct, through colonisation, the entire world as home. However, it must be noted that these are distinctions which the novel works partly to undo in the figure of the central character, the orphan Daniel Deronda, whose lack of known family origins allows for the adoption of rooted 'native' ones only to reveal his lack of rootedness in his 'foreign' Jewish origins. The novel also problematises the veneration of the 'native' family and community in its embodiment in the union of Gwendolen Harleth and Mallinger Grandcourt: whose multiplicity of homes ensure that they are at home in none; whose family is undermined by the existence of Lydia Glasher and her and Grandcourt's children; and whose relationship with each other is sterile, cruel and perfunctory.

But to return to Froude's melancholic meditation, the condition Froude articulates is that of one removed from home, an exile, a homelessness, a separation from family that ultimately implies being without family, or at least outside of it. Froude's state is metaphorically that of the orphan. It is this figure, in its literal and literary existence, and its metaphorical function, which is the focus of this book. The veneration of the family and its constitution of the nation state, is identifiable in the introduction of the *Census of 1851* by the Registrar General in which 'Marriage is generally the origin of the elementary community of which larger communities ... and ultimately the nation are constituted and on the conjugal state of the population, its existence, increase and diffusion, as well as manners, character, happiness and freedom ultimately depend', leaves the orphan as an outsider, a body without family ties to the community, a foreigner.

Before considering the orphan as a metaphor, it is necessary to consider the lived experience of the orphan during this time. There is a wealth of critical material on the fate of children of the poor from Henry Mayhew's *London's Underworld* to current critical work. This decade has seen a resurgence of interest in Victorian children of the poor (although again no specific works on orphans); the three most interesting and influential books I would argue are Carolyn Steedman's *Childhood, Culture and Class in Britain*, Hugh Cunningham's *The Children of the Poor* and Anna Davin's *Growing Up Poor*. The following chapters attempt to interweave the lived experience of the orphan with the orphan as text.

That the situation for the poor orphan was different from that of its counterpart in the bourgeoisie is perhaps obvious. One important consideration to remember however is that middle-class and wealthy custodians arranged prior to the parents' demise or departure were more likely to be able to provide for the orphan and raise him or her as their own (as in the case of Daniel Deronda), while poor orphans or deserted children were most likely to come under the control of the Board of Guardians to be raised either in a workhouse or an orphanage, or to receive outdoor relief if living with another family or relatives. The number of orphan and foundling children of poor parents was significant throughout the Victorian era. On 18 March 1844 there were a total of 18,261 children in the workhouses in England and Wales. A further 7,452 children (3,813 males and 3,339 females) had been deserted by parents in the workhouses in England and Wales (PP, 1844, XL, 235). The total relief bill as of the Census of 1841 was £4,760,929. On 1 January 1852, 40,557 children were in the workhouses in England and Wales: of these approximately 52 per cent, 21,038, were orphans or deserted children (PP, 1852, XXXIX, 1). On 1 January 1862, out of a total population of 19,774,691 (Census of 1861), there were a total of 52,125 children (27,345 boys and 24,780 girls) in the workhouses in England and Wales; of this number, 11,385 were orphans (6,043 boys and 4,388 girls) with another 1,880 children (1,061 boys and 819 girls) deserted by parents (PP, 1862, XLIX, 1). On 1 January 1877 a total of 35,187 orphans and deserted pauper children were in receipt of relief, either indoor or outdoor, in England and Wales. This was 15.2 per cent of the total number of pauper children in England and Wales at the time (PP,

1878, LXIV, 413). In a population of 22,706,302 at the Census of 1871, there were a total of 732,523 paupers (adults and children) in receipt of indoor and outdoor relief; relief which amounted to a total of £7,400,034.

For these children, more so than any of its subjects, the state stood in the place of a parent. The government and the Boards of Guardians regarded this responsibility as enshrined both within natural and canon law: these orphans and deserted children were 'made children of the State by the law and providence of God, and by the common consent and practice of all ages and nations' (preamble to the Report of the Committee on Education, PP, 1852, XXXIX, 1). In the minds of the officials, this parental duty translated into not only providing board and sustenance but also an education which would produce citizens who would contribute, E.C. Tufnell argued, 'to the useful vigour and talent of the community' (PP, 1854–55, XLII, 796), and provide both obedient citizens and a constant supply of respectable and dutiful servants. To this end, orphans in state institutions received, on average, an additional three full years of schooling, not going into service until they were thirteen, while other children of the poor went into full-time service at the age of about ten, with part-time work often starting earlier.

As the 'child' of the Poor Law Board the figure of the orphan was singularly invested with a special significance. Crucial to this significance was the fact that the orphan, as the responsibility of the Board of Guardians rather than the parents, was considered to be a figure of promise and hope. H.G. Bowyer writes in 1851 that these children were 'helpless' and thus it was the duty of society 'to emancipate them from pauperism, if possible' (PP, 1852, XXXIX, 230). A legacy from the Romantic conceptualisation of the child invested the child with an innocence; in this particular case the poor child was innocent of the causes of his or her poverty, whereas the poor adults were considered as 'reduced to destitution by their own misconduct' (PP, 1854–55, XLII, 194–5). In addition, adult poverty was perceived as a contagion of immorality. The poor adult was not only viewed as immoral and culpable but as incapable of parenting and an active source of corruption of children. E.C. Tufnell in his report to the

Committee of Education in 1854 argues that without underrating 'the good effect of rightly directed maternal influence, ... it should be remembered that we are now dealing with the lowest of the population ... Such parents either neglect their children entirely, or endeavour to lead them in the paths of honesty and vice' (PP, 1854–55, XLII, 794–5 (28–9)). Thus, the poor orphan, as one who is not under the influence of his or her allegedly immoral poor parents, provides to the Board of Guardians a *tabula rasa* – a clean slate on which they can inscribe morality, duty and a sense of place. This unique opportunity is bolstered by the fact that as an orphan receiving indoor relief (as opposed to the large number of orphans boarded out and receiving outdoor relief) this group of children would be permanent residents in the workhouse. As such, the Board of Guardians and workhouse master and mistresses, by having complete control of the environment of this group of orphan children, were able, to a great extent, to shape them – unlike the children who were only sporadically resident because their parents repeatedly committed and removed them. The Board of Guardians and the Poor Law Board perceived such children as corrupted beyond redemption by their parents. In all reports of the results of the education and training of workhouse children, responsibility for this latter class of children is repeatedly declined by the insistence that the success of the workhouse be judged on the basis of how the orphan children raised within it turned out.

Yet the orphan, as a special responsibility of the state not only offered a unique hope but also a distinct and worrying threat. 'The orphan class may turn out among the very best of the community, if properly educated. If neglected, they will, with tolerable certainty, become the worst' (PP, 1854–55, XLII, 794–5). Thus, E.C. Tufnell concluded as he tried to reconcile the fact that many orphans he came across in his years as Inspector of Parochial Union Schools took the highest honours in teaching examinations, yet simultaneously orphans furnished 60 per cent of the criminal population. In fact he reported that as of 1 January 1854, orphans constituted between 50 and 60 per cent of the population both of the pauper schools and of the Reformatory Prisons. Therefore, the nation had a strong interest in the due upbringing of poor orphans; if they were not educated they became 'thieves and paupers' whereas if they were educated they became 'well-conducted productive workpeople' (PP, 1875, LXIII, 331).

It is important to remember that almost half of the registered orphan children were female. There was the same cultural anxiety around these children as around the males, and if anything more so, because the simultaneous promise and threat that these children posed was often that embodied in the figure of Woman in Victorian culture. Of the popular narratives which sought to represent orphanhood, a number were written about female orphans. One in particular, *Susan Carter, the Orphan Girl* (1861), set in The Female Orphan Asylum, narrates a kind of workhouse ideal through the example of the protagonist, Susan Carter. Susan not only 'strove to do her duty both in word and deed' but also acted as a redemptive force in the lives of the other female orphans: 'Great good she did with her words, for many young and thoughtless mothers she was the means of reforming and making sensible and religious women; indeed, she was quite a blessing to the village' (Anon., 1861a: 74). The narrative spends a great deal of time moralising about the provision for impoverished female orphans stressing 'the incalculable blessing which a sound religious education is to the poor' (Anon., 1861a: 86). The moral of the tale is that society's failure lies in its neglect of Christian duty to its orphans by not taking responsibility for their Christian instruction (which is not surprising given that the piece is published by the Society for Promoting Christian Knowledge). The author quotes from Alexander Thomson's *Punishment and Prevention* (1856):

> God has established one great institution for training children – the family – with all its duties, its privileges, its endearments. If we are to do these children good, we must follow the plan so clearly indicated by our Heavenly Father, and endeavour to provide for them a system of training which shall, as nearly as possible, supply what they have lost – the blessing of a Christian home.

But despite the 'best intentions' in these policies for dealing with the orphan children of the poor, *The Workhouse Orphan*, a pamphlet published in 1861 by the anonymous author of *A Plea for the*

Helpless, indicts the apparent failure of the workhouse in its duty to these orphans, particularly to its female orphans. The pamphlet publishes testimony given before a Committee of Inquiry on Education in 1860 which reveals that 'all the eighty girls brought up in the Workhouse were on the streets'. The pamphlet also advertises a notice for 'The Brockman Home and Industrial Training School' whose object was to take girls aged twelve to sixteen years of age out of the workhouse both to train them as domestic servants and to provide a home to which they can return if necessary, providing that they have not committed any 'misconduct of a serious kind'. The author outlines the common plight of these female workhouse orphans; many suffer abuse by their employers while in their first job and subsequently run away. This tendency to abuse female orphan employees is succinctly expressed in the words of one employer of a young girl, sent out from the Central London district schools, 'They are only pauper girls who will gladly put up with any rough treatment.' The majority of the female orphans ended up living on the street (Vicinus, 1974; Walkowitz, 1980: 74). Not only that, but also those children who did find jobs in the community were often stigmatised and ostracised by the workhouse origins. The realisation that this Christian society was failing in its spiritual duty was one which resonated with great force. E.C. Tufnell writes: 'according as we manage the orphan destitute class, we bring a blessing or a curse on the country' (Anon., 1861b: 19).

As an experienced Inspector of Schools, Tufnell developed a preference for the orphan children of the workhouse and district schools: 'If, as sometimes happened, I have to recommend a youth or girl as a servant from a pauper establishment, I invariably choose an orphan, knowing from experience that such are the least likely to disgrace my recommendation' (PP, 1854–55, XLII, 794–5). This experience of, and personal preference for, orphan children of the workhouse and district schools forms the basis of Tufnell's objections to a report by Mrs Nassau Senior, commissioned by the Education Commission in 1872–73, which recommends the boarding out of such orphan children into homes in the community. Senior's report articulates a line of thinking objecting to the workhouse as a corrupting influence. One solution posited in her report is a more comprehensive adoption of the scheme in place in Scotland whereby orphan children would be housed and raised in families in the community. Significantly, the proposal would be more cost effective. If this were done, Tufnell argues, the entire atmosphere of the workhouse and district schools would degenerate significantly; the current positive atmosphere – which he insists characterises the majority – is due to the number of orphan children in the class who reside permanently in the workhouse and thus are subjected to 'excellent discipline' which quickly has a 'salutary influence' on them. This group of children, he argues is the 'salt of the schools' and the success of the school relies on its current composition.

> The orphans' steady conduct and good example has a powerful influence in moralising the rest of the children; ... I cannot discover that ever more than one per cent of this class fail on entering the outer world to gain an honest and independent livelihood. To remove this, the very best part of every school, is in fact to ruin it, and to consign the remainder of the children, about forty per cent of the whole to pauperism and ruin. ... Mrs Senior, with all those who advocate the boarding-out plan ... assume that all the orphans are of good character, and therefore it is shameful to mix them with the casuals, who are affected with all manners of vice [...whereas, in truth] as a rule, the orphans are quite as bad as the casuals on their admission. They become good by their permanent residence. An exception must be made in favour of those orphans who enter as infants, before they are of a corruptible age. These almost invariably turn out the best. (PP, 1875, LXIII, 323–4)

In addition to the predicted effect on the schools of a more comprehensive boarding-out scheme, opponents of this scheme argued that the domestic ideal, so important to the middle classes was, in effect, only possible in these classes. '[The supporters believe] that country cottages are readily to be found abounding in every appliance for the health, comfort, and accommodation of boarded children, and where the peasant tenants are endowed with all the motherly virtues and educational tact ... necessary to reform the vicious, enliven the apathetic, and correct the bad tempers, which ... are the common characteristics of the pauper class' (PP, 1875, LXIII, 324). However, other prominent figures, such as the Bishop of Manchester contest this view arguing that the cottages of the poor were, on the whole, 'miserable', 'deplorable', 'detestable' and 'a disgrace to a Christian community' (PP, 1875, LXIII, 324). Ironically, the same Bishop attributes this very situation to the landowners either refusing to supply decent accommodation or clearing the decent accommodation in order to provide for relatives. Whatever the reason, it cannot be forgotten that the domestic ideal required a constant supply of respectable and dutiful servants to service this myth. The main occupation for orphan children once they reached the age of thirteen was domestic service; the workhouse and district schools ensured they had the basic training for such.

In summary, it appears that there was a consensus among those most closely involved in the care of poor orphan children that: the adult poor posed a significant threat to these children; the conditions of the poor mediated against adopting a more comprehensive boarding-out policy; the orphans permanently resident in the workhouse provided a positive influence in the workhouse and district schools; and finally, that the orphan children of the poor both offered real potential for hope, yet posed a significant threat to society. In the end these arguments appeared to necessitate more drastic and interventionist action; the state was actively encouraged to make orphans of the children of the poor. By mid-century, following evidence submitted by Mr Hickson, the Committee of the House of Commons was advocating the removal of children from 'unworthy' parents (unworthy in this sense means poor and in need of relief): 'Parents who become chargeable, from whatever cause, should be considered "disenfranchised", ... no longer entitled to have control over their own children, whom the commissioners would remove by Act of Parliament to a distance of not less than three statute miles from the workhouse of which the nominal parents might be inmates' (PP, 1862, XLIX, 583). Thus, the classification system of the workhouse whereby males were housed separately from females and children separate from their parents was further extended by the adoption of district schools. Such schools originally were proposed in order to centralise the educational provision for the workhouses in the district in response to the patchy and uneven provision which existed prior to this. However, by the time of this Committee, district schools were increasingly being conceived as the mode through which 'the complete and compulsory separation of children from parents and friends' (PP, 1862, XLIX, 583) could be achieved. Thus one of the purposes of the district school came to be understood as orphaning children of the poor in order to produce malleable, useful citizens and a ready supply of domestic labour.

The paradox inherent in all this however was that while the state chose to produce orphans (or the condition of orphanhood) it was also simultaneously farming out real orphan children with local families in order to provide cheaper outdoor relief and keep the rates low. Thus, to a certain extent, the children welcomed and educated as orphans – and thus invested with a special potential – were not, while a significant proportion of real orphans were neglected, malnourished and, at best, poorly educated while boarded out. Such treatment acted as a self-fulfilling prophecy: neglect, poverty and a lack of education or training rather than immorality often turned such children to crime. Hence, the state indirectly worked to ensure that such children fulfilled their perceived potential for evil. This is one explanation why, despite the seeming concern and provision for the poor orphan, many of the poor orphan children migrated to the cities becoming part of the ever increasing numbers of homeless children in the urban areas. Such children, even more so than their urban counterparts, then became heathens beyond the reach of the state's civilising institutions. T.B. Browne, a District Inspector of Parochial Union Schools comments, as early as 1849 on the 'existence of such a class, [of children] concentrated in such vast numbers, in the manufacturing districts especially, familiarised with vice from their earliest years, ... as ignorant of religion as heathens, and reckless of moral obligation, [... This] is an evil which society, even in self-defence, appears imperatively called upon to remedy' (PP, 1850, XLIII, 189). Such children became criminals who ended up either in the Reformatory or transported.

The children who are sent to district schools represent a select class, enjoying unusual privileges. Being chiefly orphans, they are generally sent to the school early, and are always returned late. No expense or pains are spared to fit them for the higher walks of service and industry ... The selected children thus expensively brought up (at a cost of twice that of workhouse schools) and put out to places of the better class, are afterwards visited from time to time, and watched over by the chaplain or some other officer. (PP, 1862, XLIX, 1, 607)

The quotation above, from an Inspector of Parochial Union Schools, H.G. Bowyer's report of 1857, epitomises the unique opportunities the state, in its role of parent, felt it was providing for the orphan children of the poor. It is important to note that the chief endeavour of the care offered was to provide a singular opportunity to this special class of children. However, despite the claims made about the special care and attention paid to orphan children of the poor, the children – as former inhabitants of the workhouse – were stigmatised within the community at large. It was, in fact, a double bind. The Boards of Guardians of the workhouses, as legislated by the New Poor Law, were to provide board, sustenance, necessary medical attention, and some training for poor people in need of relief; they were to provide a home. Yet, simultaneously, they were not to be seen to be providing a home. No one involved in any aspect of the workhouse system would admit to providing a home, rather the workhouse was a place to be feared and to return would be seen as a disgrace. Such perceptions permeated the popular culture of the poor and working classes at the time as can be seen in 'The New Poor Law Bill in Force', a popular song in ballad form printed in broadsheets, in which the workhouse master orders that an old man and his wife be taken to the New Workhouse in a dung cart: 'Put the man in 116 cell, and the woman in 394 ward, and take the children to the barn twelve miles from there, and tell them not to let them see each other for once in two year, for we must enforce the rule of the New Poor Law Bill.' The piece opens with a general condemnation of the lack of help provided in the Poor Law Bill:

All round the country there is a pretty piece of work
All round the country against the poor people's will,
Feeble, and borne down with grief,
They ask the Parish for relief,
They tell you to go home and try to learn the Poor Law Bill.
(James, 1978: 132)

'The Workhouse and the Rich' defines the treatment of the work-house as the 'one fatal scourge invented by the rich to torture the poor' (James, 1978: 130). This perception of the workhouse as a scourge combined with the perception that it was a den of vice and iniquity, however misplaced, worked to ensure that those who came from the workhouse were often stigmatised and ostracised. This combined with the fact that the orphan children of the workhouse were continually visited and monitored until they were eighteen years of age meant that concealing their 'origin' was almost impossible. The report of a district chaplain losing his position because his workhouse origin became known was indicative of the treatment that could be expected at the hands of the community if their background was revealed. The distrust of unknown familial origins, combined with a suspicion of illegitimacy, was an experience shared by both orphans of the poor and those of the middle class. The alienation experienced by this figure is captured in the words of Miss Wade in *Little Dorrit* who, when she discovers that she is an orphan, comments: 'I carried the light of that information both into my past and into my future' (Dickens, 1953: 665).

Thus, the stigma of the workhouse which negated realisation of the very opportunities the state wished to provide for the orphan children of the poor, combined with the sharply increasing number of homeless children inhabiting the cities, posed a very real problem for those officials concerned with the welfare of these children. It was tantamount to an admission of a failure to its most vulnerable and helpless segment of the population – the orphan children – in a society that constructed its national and imperial identity around the concept of caring, responsible family values. It was seen as the failure of a Christian society to honour its Christian responsibility as articu-lated in religious teaching. *The Orphan's Friend*, a tale published by the Religious Tract Society (1842) provides an early and comprehensive overview of the Biblical teachings regarding the orphan; rather than being institutionalised, stigmatised and impoverished the orphan is to be celebrated and to share, by right, in half the produce of the land (Deut., XIV, 29; xxvi, 12, 13). As society is to be considered as a large family, the other citizens are obliged to make a feast for the orphan population (Deut., xiv, 11–14). In addition, God acts as the Father (Psa., lxviii, 5), Helper (Psa., x, 14), Judge (Psa., x, 18), Preserver (Psa., cxlvi, 9), Redeemer (Prov., xxiii, 10,11) and Witness on behalf of the orphan (Mal., iii, 5) (Anon., 1842: 27). Such teaching ensures for the orphan figure a radical provision and a spiritual authority which in no way coincided with their actual material experience and circumstance. Charles Dickens writes in 'The Haunted Man' (Dickens, 1987: 397) that 'there is not a country throughout the earth on which [the street child] would not bring a curse. There is no religion upon earth that it would not deny; there is no people on earth it would not put to shame'. However contested, the claims of Tufnell, Senior and others about the success or lack of the workhouse provision for orphan children (they were representing two schools of reform: Tufnell was in favour of removing the orphan children from the workhouse to large district schools while Senior proposing removing them from the workhouse and district schools entirely by being boarded out in the community), the early realisation that this Christian society was failing in its spiritual duty was one which resonated with great force. The rising number of those claiming relief combined with the stigma associated with receiving it, especially indoor relief, posed a very real problem for the Poor Law Commission and the Boards of Guardians: how to provide the best provision and future opportunity for the most special and vulnerable of those in their care, namely the orphans?

In response to this dilemma, the Boards turned to the colonies for a solution; as a result orphanhood takes on a new meaning: it becomes a vehicle for dispatch. As early as 1849, Boards of Guardians were considering, and in one particular case, experimenting with the idea of emigrating children of the poor, in particular orphan children, to the colonies. In his 1850 report, T.B. Browne, an Inspector of

Parochial Union Schools, argues that 'emigration is likely to become the ultimate resource of many pauper children; [... who] can easily be trained expressly to suit the purposes of colonists [... which were mainly] servants who would turn their hands to any employment, and make themselves generally useful in any emergency that might arise' (PP, 1850, XLIII, 182). Emigration was viewed by its proponents as providing orphans with a fresh start. Suddenly, the colonies rather than England were perceived as the birthright of this group of people. This scheme, however, faced opposition, but it did continue – in a much-expanded form from the early days when a few Boards of Guardians sent out selected orphan children – well into the twentieth century. This whole scheme will be considered in greater detail in Chapter 4. It is sufficient to say now that the emigration of orphan children of the poor to the colonies was paralleled by a voluntary 'migration' of certain middle-class orphans to the colonies as a way of leaving their unknown origins behind and taking up the identity of colonial workers, both policing and maintaining the boundaries of empire.

Before moving on to the chapters which consider various literary examples, a conceptual model is needed through which to understand orphanhood; the orphan figure was also symptomatic of a textual attitude. Such a model needs to be able to account for: the ambivalent attitude towards the orphan exhibited by the perception of his or her simultaneous embodiment of promise and threat; the discourses of family, indigeneity, community and native land in circulation and as expressed in the opening quotation; and the relationship between orphanhood and melancholia. Freud's notion of the uncanny as being both foreign and of the known combined with Derrida's notions of the supplementary double in which sameness always contains its difference combine in the concept *pharmakon* (a concept akin to Girard's notion of the scapegoat[2]) in which is contained simultaneously both the poison and the cure; the *pharmakon* also acts as the structure in which this difference is at one and the same time produced and excluded in order to protect the integrity of the inside. I intend to argue that the orphan plays a pharmaceutical function in Victorian culture: the orphan embodies a surplus excess to be expelled to the colonies. This expulsion works to reinforce notions of belonging in Victorian culture.

First, let us return to the quotation from *Daniel Deronda* at the opening of the chapter. In describing the early home as being marked with a 'familiar unmistakable difference', a kinship and a shared language, home and the family are delineated very much in terms of that which is known (*heimlich*) (Freud, 1987: 342); in 'The Uncanny' Freud offers definitions from several different cultures of the meaning of *heimlich*. In German, *heimlich*, meaning familiar deriving from the Latin *familiaris*, is that which 'belongs to the house, not strange, familiar, tame, intimate, friendly'; in a more general sense *heimlich* is 'belonging to the house of the family, or regarded as so belonging'. In contrast then, one outside of this family home, like the orphan, would be regarded as *unheimlich*, meaning unhomely or uncanny. In Freud's terminology the uncanny is often simultaneously associated with novelty and with fear – terms used by the Victorians themselves to define the orphan. In the English definition uncanny means, among other things, 'a repulsive fellow' (Freud, 1987: 341) while the Greek definition of uncanny means 'strange', 'foreign' and in Arabic and Hebrew uncanny means 'daemonic' and 'gruesome'. The orphan then can be read, in his or her relationship to the family and home, as occupying the same relationship of the uncanny or *unheimlich* to the *heimlich*; the orphan is unfamiliar, i.e., not of family, strange, and outside the dominant narrative of domesticity. Thus, in a narrative which, as Eliot's does, conflates individual family home with class position and national belonging, the *unheimlich* orphan comes to embody the foreigner; a 'dangerous supplement' (Derrida, 1976: 149) that comes to disturb the structure of home, identity, nation and discourse. Derrida conceives of the supplement as: 'An adjunct subaltern instance . . . . The supplement is exterior, outside of the possibility to which it is superadded, alien to that which in order to be replaced by it, must be other than it. Unlike the complement . . . the supplement is an "exterior addition"' (Derrida, 1976: 145).

Later in this book I argue that this notion of the foreigner as a 'dangerous supplement' feeds both into ambivalent narratives of domesticity (such as that found in *Wuthering Heights*) and into fear of empire (such as that found in *The Mystery of Edwin Drood*). But for the moment I would like to consider an example from *Jane Eyre*. Much has been made of Jane Eyre's orphanhood and how this leaves her as an outsider to both the Reed family and the larger community (Gilead, 1987; Plasa and Ring, 1994). Jane is constantly differentiated, excluded, and, in her own words, 'humbled by the consciousness of my physical inferiority to Eliza, John and Georgiana Reed' (Brontë, 1985: 39). Jane, for her part, continually chafes against her lack of place and status, referring to her treatment as akin to a 'rebel slave' (Brontë, 1985: 44). However, the other orphan, the 'foul German spectre – the vampire' (Brontë, 1985: 311) is the absolute outsider. Bertha, as a foreign Creole from the colonies, has no family links to the community or even to the nation. A number of critics have read Bertha as the embodiment of Jane's repressed desires; a sexual excess which needs to be contained (Gilbert and Gubar, 1979). However, this sexual excess can be read in terms of the colonial relation between the two which establishes the racialised Bertha as the illegitimate wife. Rochester's marriage to Bertha plays on both the fears of illegitimacy in the home domestic arena and the fears of miscegenation within the colonial domestic arena. As such, Bertha embodies the difference within the family (empire, nation) which needs to be excluded – and in this case eliminated – before the legitimate family can reinstate itself.

Another good example of the foreign orphan acting as a dangerous supplement is Becky Sharpe in *Vanity Fair* by William Makepeace Thackeray. From the onset we are aware of Becky's French origins and 'foreignness' in English society. Far from disabling Becky however, Becky is empowered by her French origin; e.g., she attributes her success over Miss Pinkerton to the fact that Miss Pinkerton 'doesn't know a word of French, and was too proud to confess it. I believe it was that which made her part with me; and so thank heaven for French. *Vive la France! Vive l'Empereur! Vive Bonaparte!*' (Thackeray, 1985: 47). For English society, Becky's French origins cause her to be associated with Napoleon as both an enemy and a usurper. 'In order to maintain authority in her school, it became necessary to remove this rebel, this monster, this serpent, this firebrand!' (Thackeray, 1985: 52). Thus, the orphan embodies a foreignness that is not only invasive but, as will be seen, murderous; this foreignness and the threat it poses must be excluded in order to protect the integrity of the social body.

Becky sees in her orphan status her own disadvantaged social position. The education that Becky received was that 'of shift, self, and poverty' (Thackeray, 1985: 151). But Becky's orphanhood becomes the agency through which she gains social place. Becky is constantly referring to her disadvantaged and unprotected state: 'Everybody felt the allusion ... to her hapless orphan state' (Thackeray, 1985: 73). From the subsequent pathos evoked because of her orphan status, Becky derives substantial power: 'Rebecca ... easily got the pity of the tender-hearted Amelia, for being alone in the world, an orphan without friends or kindred' (Thackeray, 1985: 54). From a young age, Becky is practising as an artist, initially as a mimic – for which she displays a natural aptitude: 'Miss Pinkerton would have raged had she seen the caricature of herself which the little mimic, Rebecca, managed to make out of her doll' (Thackeray, 1985: 50). The association of Becky with mimicry can be understood in Homi K. Bhabha's use of the term (the mimicking of the coloniser by the colonised) which gives the colonised a type of power (Bhabha, 1984: 125–33). Becky continues increasing her audience and ultimately her personal influence: "When the parties were over, ... the insatiable Miss Crawley would say, "Come to my dressing-room, Becky, and let us abuse the company" ... all of which Becky caricatured to admiration ... Miss Sharp tore them to tatters, to the infinite amusement of her audience' (Thackeray, 1985: 142). As an actress and consummate manipulator Becky eclipses all around her. This is her moment of triumph in this respect, the point at which:

> She had reached her culmination: her voice rose trilling and bright over the storm of applause and soared as high and joyful as her triumph. There was a ball after the dramatic entertainment, and everybody pressed round Becky as the great point of attraction of the evening. The Royal Personage declared, with an oath, that she

was perfection, and engaged her again and again in conversation. Little Becky's soul swelled with pride and delight at these honours; she saw fortune, fame, fashion before her ... she *écrased* all rival charmers. (Thackeray, 1985: 600–1)

But the continual masking of identity only serves to hide Becky's corrupt and threatening nature as one who is 'unsurpassable in lies' (Thackeray, 1985: 609). Finally, she murders Jos for his money.[3] It is during one of her performances that the seed of the action to follow has been planted: the murder has been foreshadowed in her earlier role playing as Clytemnestra in which she performs the murder that Aegisthus cannot: 'Rebecca performed her part so well, and with such ghastly truth, that the spectators were all dumb' (Thackeray, 1985: 596). Thus, Becky embodies a dangerous, ultimately murderous, difference throughout the novel.

However, to return to the main argument, the orphan is not truly outside the narrative of domesticity: what appears as a binary relationship hides within itself the dark secret of its own ambivalence. When explored, this ambivalence reveals that the orphan is not a foreign invading threat but is actually produced by and hence is an essential component of the family itself. In his discussion of *heimlich* Freud offers the reader an analogy between the family and a pond under which there lies a hidden spring which might reappear at any moment. Thus, in the heart of the family there is a latent living secret which might reappear at any moment thus making the family both untrustworthy and unstable. What is important in this discussion is not only that the *unheimlich* manages to make itself known and conscious, but rather that *heimlich* ultimately coincides with *unheimlich*. This ambivalence is also that which characterises the *pharmakon*. The *pharmakon* is an alien intruder or 'housebreaker' which threatens, in Derrida's terms, the 'internal purity and security' (Derrida, 1981: 128). Yet simultaneously the *pharmakon* is the structure by which this difference is 'put outside back in its place'; it is the process by which the 'excess' is eliminated (Derrida, 1981: 128) and the composition of the inside remains intact. Thus, the *pharmakon* both contains the threatening difference and is the process by which this difference is expelled.

If the *pharmakon* is 'ambivalent,' it is because it constitutes the medium in which opposites are opposed, the movement and the play that links them among themselves, reverses them or makes one side cross over into the other (soul/body, good/evil, inside/ outside, memory/forgetfulness, speech/writing, etc.). . . . The *pharmakon* is the movement, the locus, and the play: (the production of) difference. (Derrida, 1981: 127)

When applied to the family and the orphan the family is, like the Poor Law Board and the emigration societies at the time, involved in the production of orphans. The family, then, contains its opposite, in the figure of the orphan. The notion of the orphan as *unheimlich* and by that nature repressed (either discursively or through criminalisa- tion or emigration), indicates that the orphan as a figure continues to provoke in the larger family – society – fear, anxiety, guilt and inad- equacy by its presence; the anonymous author of *The Workhouse Orphan* expresses this neatly: 'If we train Pauper children as we should . . . the cry of the Orphan and oppressed will no longer rise up, in a Christian country, against those who with Christian privileges have forgotten the blessing promised to those who take care of the "widow and fatherless within their gates"' (Anon., 1861b: 25). The secret hidden nature of orphanhood manifests itself not only in foreignness but also often intertwines with illegitimacy. It is a notion that many strenuously denied at the time with regard to orphan children of the poor:

> It is a general but mistaken idea, that all Workhouse children are taken from the mere dregs of society, from the very lowest class – mostly children of shame, thirty-two girls have been taken out of different Workhouses and placed in an Orphan Home. Of these thirty-two, only two have an unknown parentage; the remaining thirty are the legitimate children of respectable parents, who had maintained them by industry and labour during their lives. (Anon., 1861b: 14)

However, far from being dismissed, the linking of orphanhood and illegitimacy persists and challenges the middle classes themselves. John Henry Newman, in *Apologia Pro Vita Sua*, asks the question: '[If I saw] a boy of good make and mind, with the token on him of a refined nature, cast upon the world without provision, unable to say whence he came, his birth-place or family connexions, I should conclude that there was some mystery connected with his history, and that he was one, of whom, from one cause or another, his parents were ashamed. Thus only should I be able to account for the contrast between the promise and the condition of his being' (Newman, 1967: 249). The question becomes even more urgent when found within the sensational novels of the middle classes about themselves. What is to be done then when faced with the question of illegitimate children who had been maintained by the industry of their respectable upper middle class parents during their lives as depicted in Wilkie Collins's novel *No Name*?

The link between orphanhood, illegitimacy and the particular problems it poses for female orphans[4] are best exemplified in Wilkie Collins's novel *No Name*. Written in the early 1860s and serialised in *All The Year Round* from 15 March 1862 to 17 January 1863, the novel follows the fortunes of two newly-orphaned sisters, Magdalen and Norah Vanstone who, on the death of their parents, discover their own illegitimacy. Written before English law was amended to allow the marriage of the parents to legitimise any children born previous to the marriage, and as a commentary on this state of affairs, *No Name* explores the special predicament of the female orphan. With the cultural anxiety around feminine sexuality (Gilbert and Gubar, 1979), female orphans, more so than male, carried the taint of the suspicion of illegitimacy. In this particular novel orphanhood and illegitimacy are conflated in that they are both revealed simultaneously. Likewise, the lack of legal status into which illegitimacy translates – namely lack of social status, lack of inheritance and the inability to possess property – is in many ways akin to the position of women in Victorian society (Collins, 1992: xix). In fact, in larger terms, this novel can be read as the disinheritance of women, orphans in particular, in Victorian culture. Ultimately, as female, orphaned and illegitimate Magdalen and Norah Vanstone find themselves literally and legally with no name. 'Mr Vanstone's daughters are Nobody's Children; ... The accident of their father having been married, when he first met with their mother, has made them outcasts of the whole social community: it has placed them out of the pale of the Civil Law of Europe' (Collins, 1992: 98). Nameless, marginalised and outside of the law, the existence of Magdalen and Norah Vanstone poses problems both for the family/state and fundamentally, for notions of self. The crux of the problem lies in the fact that their illegitimacy, revealed alongside their disinheritance on their parents' death, paradoxically arises from their parents' marriage and an outdated legal system. It is the state then and the institution of the family which relegates those who were once described as the 'priceless treasure[s] of the household' to 'castaway[s] in a strange city, wrecked on the world!' (Collins, 1992: 139). Magdalen, herself, questions the notion of self: 'Does there exist in every human being, beneath that outward and visible character which is shaped into form by the social influences surrounding us, an inward, invisible disposition, which is part of ourselves; which education may indirectly modify, but can never hope to change?' (Collins, 1992: 103–4).

But Magdalen then answers her own question a short while later by saying: 'Whether I succeed, or whether I fail, I can do myself no harm, either way I have no position to lose, and no name to degrade' (Collins, 1992: 130). For Magdalen then, identity is that which is socially constructed and familially based; lacking an identity Magdalen finds opportunity in her marginalised nameless position. Being outside the family and law, having the social constraints and respectability removed by her orphanhood and illegitimacy, Magdalen, in losing 'all care for myself' (Collins, 1992: 244), finds it possible to mask her identity and more importantly, her origins. This allows her to pursue Noel Vanstone in search of vengeance. In disguise, Magdalen talks of her own fate and warns Noel Vanstone of the vengeful Magdalen Vanstone:

> She is a nameless, homeless, friendless wretch. The law which takes care of you, the law which takes care of all legitimate children, casts her like carrion to the winds. It is your law – not hers. She only knows it as the instrument of a vile oppression, an insufferable wrong. The sense of that wrong haunts her, like a possession of the devil. ... I tell you she would resist, to the last breath in her body, the vile injustice which has struck at the help-

less children, through the calamity of their father's death! I tell you she would shrink from no means which a desperate woman can employ, to force that closed hand of yours open, or die in the attempt! (Collins, 1992: 212)

In the simultaneous masking of her identity and unmasking of her inner desire for vengeance and daemonic possession, Magdalen embodies the *pharmakon*: 'The *pharmakon* introduces and harbors death. ... Death, masks, makeup, all are part of the festival that subverts the order of the city, its smooth regulation by the dialectician and the science of being' (Derrida, 1981: 142). With her duplicity and murderous intent, Magdalen threatens the harmony of the very domestic economy which excluded her.

As *No Name* illustrates, the orphan's uncanniness then can be seen to lie in the special relationship the orphan has with the family; the orphan is a melancholic figure whose presence both embodies the loss of the family and poses problems for the discourse of family values that were structuring Victorian society and its imperial endeavours. It is a relationship which Julia Kristeva captures succinctly in her work *Strangers to Ourselves* in a passage which talks about the 'stirring mirage' which is national identity: 'our "we" is a stirring mirage to be maintained at the heart of disarray, although illusive and lacking real strength. Unless it be precisely the strength of illusion that, perhaps, all communities depend on, and of which the foreigner constantly experiences the necessary, aberrant unreality' (Kristeva, 1991: 23).

The orphan then can be read as text; a supplement in which is embodied difference within a notion of sameness. The orphan as supplement functions then in the same way that Derrida conceives of the *pharmakon* (scapegoat) which 'acts as both remedy and poison'; self-introduced 'into the body of the discourse with all its ambivalence'. As such the *pharmakon* possesses a 'power of fascination' which can be alternately or simultaneously 'beneficent or maleficent'. Yet it must be recognised as 'antisubstance itself: that which resists any philosopheme, indefinitely exceeding its bounds as nonidentity, nonessence, nonsubstance' (Derrida, 1981: 70). A slippery entity then, the orphan is: being and nonbeing; a full and empty signifier. The pharmaceutical function of the orphan is crucial in the avoidance of what critics such as Rod Edmond have termed the simplistic model of repression – liberation which has characterised a significant amount of work in Victorian studies (Edmond, 1988: 15); the *pharmakon* performs a necessary function yet somehow manages to resist analysis (a worrying prospect for one attempting to do just that) and attempts at repression.

The orphan as bane and blessing of society as embodying both good and evil, promise and threat, has a pharmaceutical function in Victorian society. Although the orphan as foreigner appears to come from the outside as can be seen from the dynamics established in Eliot's passage in its relation to the figure of Deronda himself, the *pharmakon* is of the entity (in this case the family and larger society) in which it inserts itself. The *pharmakon* is the source of the disturbance of the body – as Deronda disturbs notions of family and rootedness – as well as its remedy – it is to Deronda that Gwendolen turns for instruction and, some might argue, salvation. Thus, the *pharmakon* is both outside and of the being. In relationship to writing Derrida argues that: 'The *pharmakon* is that dangerous supplement that breaks into the very thing that would have liked to do without it yet lets itself at once, be breached, roughed up, fulfilled, and replaced, completed by the very trace through which the present increases itself in the act of disappearing' (Derrida, 1981: 110).

If we now return to *No Name* it is possible to identify the underlying mechanics as those of the *pharmakon*. Magdalen's transgressive actions, her acting and her matrimonial sacrifice to Noel Vanstone lead to the downfall of her character, but ultimately are vital for the continuance of Norah Vanstone's respectability and the reinstatement of her proper inheritance. Magdalen's embodiment of difference within is apparent from the first introduction of the two sisters. Norah Vanstone is introduced as visibly her mother's daughter: 'Her eldest child, now descending the stairs by her side, was the mirror in which she could look back, and see again the reflection of her own youth' (Collins, 1992: 4). However, Magdalen, by her looks, has no apparent genealogy:

By one of those strange caprices of Nature, which science leaves still unexplained, the youngest of Mr Vanstone's children presents no recognisable resemblance to either of her parents. How had she come by her hair? How had she come by her eyes? Even her father and mother had asked themselves those questions, as she grew up to girlhood, and had been sorely perplexed to answer them. (Collins, 1992: 5–6)

Throughout the novel the differences – physical, temperamental and moral – between the two sisters, 'so strangely dissimilar' (Collins, 1992: 46), are constantly reinforced. While Norah remains respectable and singular in the face of the loss of identity and social position, Magdalen ends up transgressive and duplicitous. From the early private theatrical in the Vanstone home of which Norah disapproves and in which Magdalen ends up playing two roles, Magdalen embodies a doubleness and a difference which ultimately is pharmaceutical in function: it allows the exploration of difference, but ultimately it is to be excluded. It can be argued then that Norah's respectability and final familial inheritance is based on Magdalen's transgressive actions/acting. In the same way that the racialised colonial other functions to reinstate the imperial self (as was seen in the function of Bertha in *Jane Eyre*), in *No Name* the transgressive female shores up the respectable family.

In summary then, the orphan's very presence is both vital to and a disruption of notions of being – particularly home, nation, discourse and writing. The orphan then performs a paradoxical function: he or she is both redemptive and a threat. The latter often manifests itself in the body of the criminal. While the former was seen as a cause for celebration the latter is subject to a mode of discursive control. Both the relationships, as redeemer and criminal, demonstrate that although the orphan as *pharmakon* displays a certain amount of power it is a figure comprehended in the structure of Victorian England.

Although the model is a persuasive one,[5] it is not applied rigidly in the following chapters, but used to offer a mode of understanding the profound ambivalence regarding the representation of the orphan figure during this time. Although Freud and Derrida produce very suggestive models for understanding the representation of the orphan figure, I do not adopt the underlying psychoanalytic or post-structuralist methodologies in my interpretative approach. The book's structure moves from a consideration of the problems to which the presence of the orphan figure gave rise to the attempts to expel orphans to, finally, the orphan's return in various literary texts. In Chapter 2, I establish a discursive context in which to read the orphan figure as embodying a difference within the family. To do so, I read the figure of Heathcliff in *Wuthering Heights* against a number of discourses – namely, those of the foundling, the orphan as foreigner, and the orphan as criminal. Chapter 3 looks at the role of the orphan and popular orphan adventure narratives in policing and extending empire. Here I consider Charles Dickens's 'The Perils of Certain English Prisoners, and Their Treasure in Women, Children, Silver and Jewels' (Dickens, 1987) within the context of both the Indian Mutiny of 1857 and Dickens's own imperial sympathies. Chapter 4 offers the historical context for the schemes adopted at the time for emigrating orphans. I focus on the three main destinations – Bermuda, New South Wales and Canada – in order to consider the motivations behind the emigrating of orphans and the contemporary evaluations of it. In this historical context, I position Rose Macaulay's *Orphan Island* (1924), which in its Utopian framework poses problems for the both the rationale of the schemes and for current debates within post-colonial studies. Chapter 5 looks at the exiling of difference, in George Eliot's *Daniel Deronda* and the return of the exiled orphan from the colonies to the heart of empire, London, in Dickens's *The Mystery of Edwin Drood*.

2

Difference within

You must e'en take it as a gift of God; though it's as dark almost as
if it came from the devil. (Brontë, 1968: 41)

THE INTRODUCTION of Heathcliff into the Earnshaw
family at Thrushcross Grange is one which establishes an
initial binary relationship between the orphan and the
family by inscribing within the figure of the orphan Heathcliff an
absolute difference. The difference Heathcliff embodies is so
absolute that he makes his first appearance as a 'dirty, ragged, black-
haired child' who articulates his difference outside the language of
the family when he speaks 'some gibberish that nobody could understand'. He is quickly labelled as a 'gipsy brat' who receives a less than
warm welcome into the Earnshaw family: Mrs Earnshaw flies into a
rage and queries Mr Earnshaw's sanity; Nellie was frightened;
Hindley 'blubbers aloud' when the same great coat that produced
Heathcliff has crushed his fiddle 'to morsels'; Cathy spits at
Heathcliff on discovering that her present of a whip was lost when
her father attended 'the stranger' Heathcliff. Thus, Heathcliff, by his
entrance, disrupts the domestic harmony and in so doing triggers a
violent reponse. Mrs Earnshaw quickly establishes Heathcliff as
other to 'their own bairns' who they had 'to feed and fend'; it is a
statement which quickly delineates the parameters and priorities of
the family. Nellie and the children through their actions refuse
Heathcliff status as a human; he is metamorphosed by their actions
and discursive representation as a dog. The children refuse to allow
'it' into their bedroom; Nellie puts 'it on the landing of their stairs' in

the desperate hope that 'it might be gone on the morrow' (Brontë, 1968: 41–2). It remains to be seen however, whether Heathcliff is to become the dog that the Linton children almost pull apart between them or the bulldog Skulker who is pulled from his hold of Cathy's ankle with 'his huge purple tongue hanging half a foot out of his mouth, and his pendant lips streaming with bloody slaver' (Brontë, 1968: 54–5). Demonised and dehumanised from the onset, and embodying, in his dark features, the mark of difference, Heathcliff disturbs the family narrative: 'from the very beginning, he bred bad feeling in the house; and at Mrs Earnshaw's death … the young master [Hindley] had learnt to regard his father as an oppressor rather than a friend, and Heathcliff as a usurper of his parent's affections, and his privileges, and he grew bitter with brooding over these injuries' (Brontë, 1968: 42–3).

Recent considerations of *Wuthering Heights*, such as Terry Eagleton's *Heathcliff and the Great Hunger*, have situated the figure of Heathcliff in the context of the (im)migration of the Irish poor caused by the potato famine; Eagleton identifies the gibberish as Celtic and the fact that Heathcliff was discovered in Liverpool, one of the main cities to which the Irish migrated during the famine, as evidence of Heathcliff's Irish ancestry. Other critics read Heathcliff as embodying the racial difference of empire (Perera, 1991; Meyer, 1996). In fact, the racialised representation of the Irish during the time (cf., Innes, 1990) does allow for the conflation of these two into a generalised racialised difference embodying a colonial difference which erases cultural specificity. This is a feature of the operation of orientalist and colonialist discourses. Without taking direct issue with these arguments, I extend the context of the positioning further by reading Heathcliff in light of a strand of popular writing which narrativises the orphan figure as embodying difference within Victorian culture. For my purposes, there are three identifiable strategies used to construct difference within these popular orphan narratives: the mysterious foundling with seemingly no known origins; the association of the orphan figure with travelling peoples (gypsies) who, by their lifestyle, disrupt certain notions of rootedness, family, home, Christianity and nationhood; and the criminalised orphan figure. Before considering Heathcliff in more detail, I will offer a representative example of each of these three types of narrative in order to explore the concern with the orphan figure in these types of popular writing. Then I intend to consider the figure of Heathcliff within this context as an embodiment of these types to argue that *Wuthering Heights* can be read not so much as the strange product of an isolated young woman writer but as an intertextual piece of writing concerned with narrativising anxieties about belonging and foreignness as related to the home, class and national identity.

The mysterious foundling

In 1842, Leapidge Smith edited a reprint of a 1643 Oxford legend (*The Orphan; The Foundling; Abiah*) entitled *Abiah, Or, The Record of a Foundling* in order to raise money for a foundling child discovered in Newgate Market in May 1842. The choice of such a tale to benefit a real foundling is obvious but it is also the choice of a tale which identifies foundling children (those abandoned by their parents) with orphan children (those children who have no parents) in an act of effacement of familial responsibility in which the family articulates its own supplementary difference. The supplementary nature of this difference is that it is the family which expels the orphans that it produces/contains. The supplement is ambivalent in its function – excluding that which threatens the 'inside'/internal security' of the family by putting the outside out, in a position of illegitimacy. Significantly, foundling literature, in its association with issues of illegitimacy and familial intrigue (mystery) is most often used to represent middle-class orphan figures: figures who by virtue of their class position are the most likely to be recuperated. It is also an act of manifesting the loss of family not only literally but also psychologically. It can be understood then as a narrative that articulates the melancholic nature of this figure who, by its very presence, acts as a continual remembrance of the event of loss. At times this figure then becomes indistinguishable from the cause of the loss. Such representation carries the potential to generate a profound effect on a society centred on familial responsibility and the orphan's self-identity. The linkage between the orphan and the family then serves to identify both as melancholic structures that embody loss. The reprint of the Oxford legend is careful to conform to the organising sensibilities in early Victorian popular foundling and orphan literature, namely: the unknown parentage (originary mystery); the threatened inheritance (on both literal and metaphorical levels of name, place and essentialised discourses of identity which see identity as something inherent and transmittable); and the final revelation of a long-lost legacy. The latter point demonstrates not only the anxiety this figure causes to the family but the tremendous need of this same family to erase its doubleness by recouping this figure and hence neutralising the difference he embodies. Thus, it is possible to identify the supplement's positive connotation in its redemptive character: by recouping the orphan, the family, which is under threat, is able to reinstate and reaffirm itself.

In *Abiah, Or, The Record of a Foundling*, which comprises three short poems (on orphanhood, foundling child and Abiah) and a narrative, the central character Abiah is the child of the marriage of the master of the manor and his true love Miss St Maur. Just after Abiah is conceived the master dies suddenly. Both Miss St Maur and her new born child are objects of envy for the master's younger brother who has had his succession to the estate and lands removed by the marriage and the production of an heir. While Miss St Maur is weak recovering from childbirth, the disreputable younger brother-in-law sets fire to the home with the intention of killing both St Maur and her new-born child, thus restoring what he perceives as his rightful position as heir. The mother perishes in the fire but the child is rescued by a faithful servant and sent to the St Maur family home with another servant. On the way, the servant entrusted with the care of the child is killed and the child, now named Abiah, is raised as a foundling. Ultimately, Abiah's true parentage is discovered and he claims his rightful family name, inheritance and social place.

The significance of the name given to the foundling, Abiah meaning the 'Lord is my Father' gives to the unknown origins a spiritual dimension. These spiritual resonances tap a residual Romantic legacy in which the child was conceived as 'trailing clouds of glory' in his recent arrival from his spiritual home. It was a legacy that emphasised the orphan's spiritual genealogy. It is an explicit attempt to counteract the distrust of such a figure that often, as in the case of *Silas Marner*, translates into a demonisation of the orphan as threatening, foreign, outsider: 'How was a man to be explained unless you at least knew somebody who knew his father and his mother?' (Eliot, 1985: 51). The final poem of the collection entitled 'Abiah' emphasises the Christian responsibility articulated also by Mr Earnshaw at the moment of introducing Heathcliff; these children were to be understood to have a full membership within the larger spiritual family and a father in the figure of God. In emphasising the shared spiritual genealogy the narrative seeks to obfuscate the singular difference under erasure by subsuming it into a grand narrative of the Christian family. In doing so, the orphan is constructed as both a figure of pathos and the particular responsibility of the larger society which professes to be a Christian one.

> No parent owns Abiah here,
> No home Abiah claims to share;
> No father's love, no Mother's glory,
> A Foundling Child is his sad story.
>
> Say not, he has no Father's love;
> There's One who dwells in heaven above,
> Whose love is love beyond all others,
> Stronger than the love of mothers.
> Father's and mother's may forsake,
> But his will never, never break;
> The Parent of the fatherless!
> Their shelter and refuge in distress!
> Here may Abiah claim a home,
> More precious than an earthly one;
> A happy home in heaven above,
> Safe in the arms of Jesus' love;
> Nor sad the little Foundling's story,
> Who thus attains a home of glory.
> (Smith, 1842: 9)

Thus, it is possible to read *Abiah, Or, The Record of a Foundling* as representative of a strand within popular writing which aligns the foundling child with the orphan. It is a strand of writing which is both anxious and ambivalent about the status of both the family and the orphan's supplementary nature to this family as both good and bad, an outsider-in to be excluded.

The demonisation of such a figure highlights this ambivalence felt towards the orphan figure: in the tale Abiah's difference manifests itself in his 'uncommon clothing' and 'singular characteristics', which appear 'quite natural in him exhibiting a marked difference from the other child reared at the same breast' (Smith, 1842: 4). Thus, even sharing the same mother's milk, which Eliot identifies as so important, cannot erase the essentialised difference between those of the family and those that are not. This difference then forms the basis of Abiah's exclusion from the very familial structure which produced him: 'degrees and orders were beyond his reach'; 'He had to meet the silent scorn of the proud and noble vulgar! In the midst of society he was alone! lonely! ... There is a void in his heart which nothing seems calculated to fill' (Smith, 1842: 18–19). Ultimately, unlike the orphan, the discovery of Abiah's rightful family name ends his enforced marginalisation restoring him to a social place and membership of the larger society.

The association of the orphan with travelling peoples

The second strand of writing, namely that in which the orphan is linked, however tenuously, to travelling peoples, is an exploration of a marginalised difference to be found within society and which starts to articulate difference through racial, ethnic and sectarian terms. Mootoo's (pseudonym) *The Orphan: A Romance*, published in 1850, is an interesting tale. The title itself is of particular significance in its signalling the writer's adoption of the conventions of romance to represent the orphan figure. The move away from the realism dominating this kind of writing to romance is one to note. In undertaking the project of romance, as opposed to realism, the author would be signalling to her contemporary audience that her project was not what Nathaniel Hawthorne termed an act of 'minute fidelity' but rather of a more fantastic nature. The romance opens up the possibility of dealing with allegorised archetypes (Frye, 1957: 306) which is important to keep in mind when considering this tale.

The Orphan: A Romance is about the life of Squire Hawthorn's son who is sold to gypsies by the Squire's evil brother Caleb in order that Caleb may claim the family inheritance. The tale narrates the child's life with these gypsies. When the old gypsy Reginald finally confesses to what has taken place, the orphan is restored to his rightful family estate and inheritance. There are several things to note in this allegorical tale. The narrative in its consideration of the life of the orphan with the gypsies works to establish the travelling peoples and their culture as Other: the gypsies are constructed as savage heathens and demonised as a corrupting threat to the 'civilised' members of society as represented by their willingness to work with corrupt elements within the mainstream society to destroy the family unit by subverting the line of familial succession. The gypsies have no hesitation in purchasing or even stealing children away from their families; yet paradoxically, having worked to destroy one family, the gypsies form another by raising the child as their own. The gypsies are represented as barbarous and corrupt but they work in conjunction with truly corrupt and barbarous elements within the society – in the figure of the uncle willing to sell his nephew in order to steal his inheritance. The root of the threat is twofold. The existence of the gypsies within (albeit on the margins of) Victorian England and the racialised difference they embody poses uncomfortable problems for the construction of Victorian society as a family. Homelessness and a travelling lifestyle disrupt a family narrative and established social structures. But even more difficult for this construction is the existence within the heart of this society of elements, like the uncle, who seek to disrupt the family narrative, do not respect the bonds of family, and display traits antithetical to the civilised values which the society used to distinguish itself from barbarous cultures. The allegorical project of this romance is most clearly identifiable in the figure of the orphan child who retains the essential qualities of purity and morality claimed by the society as its own even while being raised by gypsies. The retention of such traits allows this child to assume his rightful inheritance espousing the values of rootedness, family and Christianity – all component values of the English subject.

The criminal orphan

The third strand of writing concerns itself with exploring the process by which the orphan is criminalised; the orphan population comprised some sixty per cent of the population of the reformatories. Estimates of how many orphan children were to be found among the burgeoning number of street children in urban areas are imprecise, but most agree that there were thousands. The destiny of a large number of orphan children, including a number of workhouse orphans, to become criminals is a testament to the neglect suffered by many of them. In *The Workhouse Orphan*, the pamphlet written in response to the 1860 Committee of Inquiry on Education, the author, in reviewing the current state of the New Poor Law provision, argues that the institutions for the care of the poor, particularly the orphan children of the poor, are still failing in their duty. Orphan children living on the street were most likely to be criminalised both by need and by association. Once on the street the author argues that 'they were all lost characters; old in vice, though still young in years' (Anon., 1861b: 10). The destiny of most orphans to become criminals as a direct result of the abuse and lack of care they received raises the question of whether this society was actively producing and criminalising orphans.

The whole issue of the orphaned children of the poor is a poignant and emotive one; the state, in failing to provide adequately for the future of these children is failing in the especial responsibility invested in it. The orphan child is a figure of special pathos: 'Is there any child more weak and helpless than a Workhouse Orphan?' (Anon., 1861b: 15). The author queries whether it can be 'right, then, to consider them as outcasts and treat them as if they were not belonging to that one great family of which Christ is the head?' (Anon., 1861b: 15). As in *Abiah, Or, The Record of a Foundling*, the

37

author of *The Workhouse Orphan* argues for a more comprehensive religious instruction for orphans as compensation: 'though Forsaken by earthly parent, they [the orphans] have a Father in Heaven' (Anon., 1861b: 15). The presence of the orphan then haunts the social psyche: 'the cry of the Orphan and oppressed ... rises up, in a Christian country, against those who with Christian privileges have forgotten the blessing promised to those who take care of "the widow and fatherless within their gates"' (Anon., 1861: 25).

The criminalisation of the orphaned children of the poor and the sense of social failure the existence of such orphan criminals generates within the middle-class psyche gives rise to a mode of narrating the orphan which I term 'penal narrative'. The orphan criminal is often a product of family neglect; the author quotes the remorseful last words of a dying orphan 'I have been very wicked, but no one ever taught me better, no one ever cared for me' (Anon., 1861b: 27). The penal narrative, as evidenced in the title of Alexander Thomson's *Punishment and Prevention* (1856), is one in which the orphan is a potential unruly member in need of a constant Foucauldian type of discipline by the family. Mrs Sheppard, author of *Sunshine in the Workhouse*, argues that:

> The Workhouse Orphan has no friend to take him by the hand and remind him that there is an All-Seeing Eye ever upon him, a tender and loving Father above, who is grieved when his children disobey His commandments, and who will help him do better if he asks Him. He is at once condemned as a wicked boy, he becomes hardened to all good feelings, and is soon the willing companion of regular thieves, reckless in evil, feeling that he is an outcast in the world. (Thomson, 1856: 18)

The author warns that the workhouse's failure to undertake the responsibility of the family produces the orphan as an outcast. The mode of narrating the orphan as undisciplined and the role of the family as disciplinary establishes the penal narrative. Alexander Thomson argues: 'God has established one great institution for training children – the family' (Thomson, 1856: 11–12). Thomson's larger argument is interesting for its explicit identification of the role of Victorian society, and thus its representative institutions, as a parental one. Thus, the workhouse needs both to act as a home and to play a moral, parental role in the lives of its orphan inmates if it is to be effective in the instruction of its inmates in a virtuous lifestyle.

Perhaps the most dangerous element of the conceptualisation of the orphan as criminal is when the orphan is represented as existing in 'a torpor of both the mental and physical system' in which 'Memory and hope, two of God's best gifts to man, and as precious to the poor as to the rich, are unknown to the Workhouse Orphan' (Anon., 1861b: 13). The lack of memory and hope is in effect condemning the orphan to a perpetual present outside of history as past (memory) and future (hope) do not exist. In such a conception, the orphan is static – an ahistorical figure outside of the narrative of progress. Such a state of continual present dooms the orphan child to extinction; s/he exists outside of the narrative of history-as-progress. The orphan shares the static qualities of this conceptualisation with that of racial others who were viewed as 'inferior' because they were thought incapable of development. Such conceptualisation was necessary in order to neglect the orphan so; the conception of the orphan as a figure not rooted in tradition as an organising force for progress enables the orphan to be mistreated. This conceptualisation makes the orphan vulnerable to a number of fates: death by misadventure or neglect; or the 'cleansing' of society by getting rid of the orphan through transportation, emigration or capital punishment.

Oliver Twist and the criminal orphan narrative

Published in 1838, *Oliver Twist* is perhaps one of the best known criminal orphan narratives. In fact, Dickens wrote *Oliver Twist* as an attempt to counteract the glamour of the Newgate novels, in order to 'dim the false glitter surrounding something which really did exist and to show it in its unattractive and repulsive truth' (1841 Preface, p.lxiv). The term Newgate novels refers to a number of popular narratives of the time which were seen to glamorise the criminal underworld. In setting out to 'draw a knot of such associates … as really do exist; to paint them in all their deformity, in all their wretchedness, in all the squalid poverty of their lives' (1841 Preface, p.lxii), Dickens wants to show the grim reality of the criminal under-world with which Oliver, as an unprotected orphan, comes into contact. I want to examine this tale as a number of popular criminal orphan narratives were based on *Oliver Twist*.

Oliver, described by Dickens in his 1841 Preface as the 'principle of Good', is in continual confrontation with adversity, corruption and ill treatment, arising out of his contact with various social institutions. *Oliver Twist* is a loosely structured allegory which is reinforced by the subtitle, *The Parish Boy's Progress*. Dickens chooses a child, specifically an orphan, for both the principal character in this moral tale and the embodiment of the 'principle of Good'. To the family, this orphan figure is also a figure of special pathos. Hence, the trials undergone by Oliver arising primarily from his lack of family are especially potent for the Victorian reader.

From the moment of Oliver's birth when there is 'nobody by' (Dickens, 1966: 1), Oliver experiences alienation and loneliness – experiences that define the orphan as outsider and scapegoat. Because of his lack of family, Oliver is identified by the workhouse – the institution which can be read as having produced him: 'He was badged and ticketed, and fell into his place at once – a parish child – the orphan of a workhouse – the humble half-starved drudge – to be cuffed and buffeted through the world – despised by all, and pitied by none' (Dickens, 1966: 3). The workhouse scenes serve to underline Oliver's enforced isolation, epitomised by his imprisonment – the language of which is akin to that of the solitary confinement of a prisoner. 'For a week after the commission of the impious and profane offence of asking for more, Oliver remained a close prisoner in the dark and solitary room to which he had been consigned' (Dickens, 1966: 12). Oliver possesses a heightened awareness of his loneliness: 'A sense of his loneliness in the great wide world, sank into the child's heart' (Dickens, 1966: 8). The orphan is seen as an outsider deeply troubled by his status of outsider and his resulting lack of sense of community. The social institutions which are supposed to be taking care of him in actuality are producing orphans rather than acting as parental substitutes.

Also, it is through these social institutions that the penal narrative is developed and inscribed on the orphan. This loneliness and lack of belonging is increased at Sowerberry's, until Oliver fervently wishes for his own death, as a relief from the misery and profound loneliness of his life:

> Nor were these the only dismal feelings which depressed Oliver. He was alone in a strange place ... The boy had no friends to care for, or to care for him. The regret of no recent separation was fresh in his mind; the absence of no loved and well-remembered face sunk heavily into his heart ... he wished, as he crept into his narrow bed that was his coffin ... that he could be laid in a calm lasting sleep in the churchyard ground: with the tall grass waving gently above his head: and the sound of the old deep bell to soothe him in his sleep. (Dickens, 1966: 26)

However, Oliver does not get his wish for death granted as he lies in his coffin, instead he becomes a figure of living death in the form of the child mute. Subsequently, Fagin, Mr Brownlow and the house-keeper are all struck by the innocence Oliver's countenance reflects; it is indirectly through Oliver's countenance that the secret of his parentage is made known. Oliver's familial identity will continue to insist upon its own recognition through his distinctive features, eventually resulting in his reintegration into the family. The essentialised nature of this recognition could be interpreted as racial. Oliver's features are distinctive of a racial belonging and this allows for his reassimilation – unlike the racialised working-class orphans and the street 'arabs' who are orientalised to embody a racial otherness within Victorian society. This is certainly the case with Monks whose dark features, strange fits, and 'bad' disposition serve to emphasise his difference. This difference is threatening to Oliver's familial belonging and the family economy which seeks to reassimilate him. Oliver's essential family identity allows him to resist the other narratives offered to him, which seek to give him another identity (that of parish child, child mute, criminal) by successively fleeing each repressive institution or social situation (excluding Mr Brownlow's) – as he does initially in the case of the Sowerberry's when 'his spirit was roused at last' (Dickens, 1966: 37).

Throughout his trials, however, Oliver does manage to retain his innocence and his inherent faith by refusing to participate either in the official institutional narrative forced on him, or in the criminal narrative that Monks so desperately wants to thrust upon him. In his desperation, Oliver turns to his 'Father' for protection. 'He prayed to Heaven to spare him from such deeds; and rather to will that he should die at once, than be reserved for crimes, so fearful and appalling ... he stood alone in the midst of wickedness and guilt' (Dickens, 1966: 130). It is very significant to note that Dickens's portrayal of criminality is a portrait of destitution – both physical and moral – neglect, corruption, and misery:

> Countenances, expressive of almost every vice in almost every grade ... cunning, ferocity, and drunkenness in all its stages, were there, in their strongest aspects; and women ... with every mark and stamp of their sex utterly beaten out, and presenting but one loathsome blank of profligacy and crime: some mere girls, others but young women, and none past the prime of life: formed the darkest and saddest portion of this dreary picture. (Dickens, 1966: 164)

The fact that Oliver shares this destitution, misery and alienation makes him a criminal by association. Fagin tries to make him an actual criminal by '[letting] him feel that he is one of us ... [and filling] his head with the idea that he has been a thief (Dickens, 1966: 126). But in this case, as in all others, Oliver resists the inner process of criminalisation, the descent into vice, because of his inherently pure nature – a nature which resists this process of moral corruption. Hence, Oliver's countenance still pays tribute to his innocent nature and he epitomises the 'principle of Good'. So while Dickens does acknowledge that his society, through neglect, is a factor in the criminalisation of certain sectors of the population, Dickens still empowers Oliver, through a Romantic aesthetic construction of innocence, to resist becoming 'A thief, a liar, a devil: all that's bad, from this night forth' (Dickens, 1966: 104), and hence, to resist the penal narrative. Throughout his trials, Oliver retains a nobility of purpose which, indirectly, will lead to his own salvation from evil. 'The boy had firmly resolved that, whether he died in the attempt or not, he would make one effort to dart up stairs from the hall, and alarm the family' (Dickens, 1966: 145). Finally, it is Oliver's heroic attempt to overcome his own loneliness, even on the verge of death, that leads to his reintegration into a family. 'It would be better he thought, to die near human beings, than in the lonely, open fields' (Dickens, 1966: 183). So, on one hand, part of Oliver's role is to reflect the state of various social institutions, as David Miller argues: 'Oliver moves from one institution to another with extraordinary ease – from workhouse, to family, to "flash-house", back to the family and so on; in doing so he becomes an empty signifier who merely demonstrates the proliferation of such institutions.'[6]

Ultimately, Oliver is integrated into both a family and the larger community. Mr. Brownlow becomes his father. 'Mr Brownlow adopted Oliver as his own son ... he gratified the only remaining wish of Oliver's warm and earnest heart, and thus linked together a little society, whose condition approached as nearly to one of perfect happiness as can ever be known in this changing world' (Dickens, 1966: 365).

A good example of popular literature narrativising this state of affairs is Miss E. Matthews' *The Orphan Boy; or, How Little John was Reclaimed* (1863) which blatantly plagiarised Dickens's *Oliver Twist*. Like *Oliver Twist* this tale voiced a cultural anxiety around the fact that children, and orphans in particular, were being gradually criminalised through neglect. The plot is easily recognisable – John's mother Mary dies and with her dies the idealised working-class home. John's father, also named John, remarries a widow. The widow is a stereotypical cruel stepmother figure who ill-treats and even beats John. John's father falls into drunkenness and eventually dies – this death is portrayed as a fitting punishment for failing to protect his son and falling victim to the vice of drunkenness. In this second home the working-class father is demonised as corrupt and abusive, whose vice and lifestyle destroy the family unit. Again the familial ideal is seen as the preserve of the middle classes. Through neglect and desperation, Little John falls in with thieves who are under the control of Jolly Bob, a Fagin-like character.

You can't expect that 'Jolly Bob'
Will keep us both in food,
Unless we take him something home,
As thieves in honour should.

He's taught us all the tricks we know;
You're quite as quick as me;
And why you fear to make a snap,
I really cannot see.
(Matthews, 1863: 9)

The narrative works to demonise street children as a criminal threat precisely because their incorporation into a surrogate criminal family poses problems for the ideal of the family; the existence of such criminalised children implies the family, and the state, is in crisis. As an idealised child the original product of an idealised family, Little John displays the same inherent revulsion to crime as Oliver Twist does, but in Little John's case this is overcome. Miss Matthews is obviously determined to illustrate that this environment is ultimately corrupting, producing criminalised orphans. Little John's ability to retain his innocence in this environment for almost five years identifies him as a worthy subject for recuperation into the social family. Eventually, Little John is detected stealing a pocketbook and a chase scene, derived from *Oliver Twist*, ensues:

But hark! What sound is that he hears
Borne faintly on the mind?
'Stop thief' – John rushes madly on,
While steps are heard behind.

With cries and yells the crowd pursue,
They nearer, nearer come;
He rushes now with flying speed
To reach his distant home.

Tis vain, the thief is caught at last,
A policeman holds him tight,
And takes him to the Station-house,
To linger for the night.
(Matthews, 1863: 12)

Unlike Oliver, Little John spends one month in jail – as an indication that he has been fully criminalised. The time in prison acts as a process of internal reformation exemplified by his rediscovered 'honest impulses'. On his release, Little John anguishes about what to do; he is revolted by his criminal life. Here, Miss Matthews, rather obviously, addresses the readership about the plight of the orphan. In the figure of Little John, Miss Matthews insists on the idealised nature of the orphan who is criminalised by neglect. John's turning to crime out of necessity then is a microcosm of the general plight of the orphan.

> Poor children that had never known
> A parent of a friend;
> He reach'd the gates, then paus'd to think.
>
> 'If I go back to Bob,' he said,
> 'He'll make me steal and lie;
> And if I roam about the streets,
> I shall with hunger die.'
>
> It may be so, but let me ask,
> Where shall the outcast go?
> The thief, the wanderer, whom the world
> In scorn will never know?
> (Matthews, 1863: 13)

Like Oliver, Little John's innocent nature is reflected in his features. Such physiognomy can be understood in racial terms as signifying racial belonging and thus differentiating him from others. Once again, these features catch the attention of a passing benevolent gentleman who notices Little John's 'honest face' (Matthews, 1863: 15) and the signs of an inward struggle. This gentleman subsequently decides to befriend Little John. John grows up a pious Christian father who uses the story of his life in his teaching of his children.

In all of the tales above, the figure of the orphan, without exception, signifies an otherness. This otherness takes two forms: the pathetic other in need of patronage; or the orientalised[7] other representing difference within Victorian society. The narrative not only represents the attempt to recoup and assimilate the orphan figure but also the fact that the family structure is under pressure.

Wuthering Heights and popular orphan narratives

So from the discovery of Heathcliff 'starving, and houseless, and as good as dumb in the streets of Liverpool' (Brontë, 1968: 41–2), it is possible to read in Heathcliff the three central narratives identified in the popular narratives. Like the popular orphan narratives, this narrative constructs Heathcliff's difference through both the lack of known origins and the association of Heathcliff with travelling peoples (gypsies) – whose presence on the margins of Victorian society pose problems for the society's self-identity as rooted in family, place and Christianity.

Initially, Heathcliff appears as the mysterious foundling discovered on the streets of Liverpool and taken under the protection of Mr Earnshaw. A preliminary investigation fails to discover from whence he came; from the moment of his arrival at Wuthering Heights, Heathcliff appears to have no known or discernible origins. The act of naming Heathcliff simultaneously enshrines his orphanhood and lack of familial genealogy, by having a single name Heathcliff as both Christian name and surname. In naming Heathcliff after the son who died in childhood (Brontë, 1968: 42) the family recognises in Heathcliff a lost member; he is not seen as removed from the family but as existing within the economy of the family, a supplement which embodies the difference within, an outsider-in. This can be understood as a moment of recuperation/recognition by the family. Although there is recognition, a sense of mystery surrounds Heathcliff throughout his life from his arrival in the Earnshaw family to the source of his new-found wealth on his return. This sense of mystery extends to his very nature as well.

Although Heathcliff is named through an act of recuperation, he is constructed as the embodiment of the difference within which takes the form of an enforced marginalisation from the family based on his orphanhood. When Isabella writes to Nelly and asks, 'Is Mr Heathcliff a man? If so, is he mad? And if not, is he a devil? ... I beseech you to explain, if you can, what I have married' (Brontë, 1968: 148–9), she feeds the widespread distrust of Heathcliff which has arisen from his unknown origins; Heathcliff's very humanity is questioned. Isabella uncovers Heathcliff's 'devilish nature' and refers to Heathcliff as a 'monster [who needs to be blotted] ... out of memory' (Brontë, 1968: 189); in the end she insists that Heathcliff is 'not a human being' (Brontë, 1968: 89).

Throughout his existence at Wuthering Heights, Heathcliff is constructed as inhuman and devilish. His lineage is assumed to be with 'kin beneath' (Brontë, 1968: 190) [a family of devils]; he is referred to as a 'hellish villain' (Brontë, 1968: 192), an 'evil genius ... gaunt and ghastly' (Brontë, 1968: 196), by implication a cannibal ('his mouth watered to tear you with his teeth; because, he's only half a man – not so much' (Brontë, 1968: 197)) who laughs 'a fiendish laugh' (Brontë, 1968: 238). Joseph implies that Heathcliff has murdered Hindley (Brontë, 1968: 203); Heathcliff is viewed as a 'detected villain' (Brontë, 1968: 252), a 'devil' (Brontë, 1968: 307), a 'diabolical man' (Brontë, 1968: 241). Indeed Heathcliff is profoundly unloved which has made him 'lonely, like the devil and envious like him' (Brontë, 1968: 309; young Catherine tells him 'Nobody loves you – nobody will cry for you, when you die! I wouldn't be you!' (Brontë, 1968: 309); a devil who lives in an 'earthly hell' (Brontë, 1968: 350) and who 'had a delight in dwelling on dark things' (Brontë, 1968: 349). Heathcliff acknowledges that all around him see him as a 'fiend ... something too horrible to live under a decent roof!' (Brontë, 1968: 360). On his deathbed the devil claims him as his own ('Th' divil's harried off his soul ... what a wicked un he looks grinning at death!' (Brontë, 1968: 361)). For Nelly, death has transformed Heathcliff from a fiend to a goblin whose role will become that of haunting: 'Those deep black eyes! That smile, and ghastly paleness! It appeared to me, not Mr Heathcliff, but a goblin; and, in my terror, I let the candle bend towards the wall, and it left me in darkness' (Brontë, 1968: 354).

This construction of Heathcliff has a twofold function: his devilish and evil nature works to identify him as a usurper, a threat to the established family genealogy: 'He must have had some ups and downs in life to make him such a churl. Do you know anything of his history?' 'It's a cucioo's; sir – I know all about it; except where he was born, and who were his parents, and how he got his money, at first – And Hareton has been cast out like an unfledged dunnock – The unfortunate lad is the only one, in all this parish, that does not guess how he has been cheated!' (Brontë, 1968: 39). Secondly, this construction gives him a pharmaceutical function – his presence and the necessity to exclude it work as a cure to what ails the family economy. Heathcliff is threatening to the family when he, for example, encourages Hindley's depraved lifestyle making him 'worse and worse' as 'they sit up all night together' (Brontë, 1968: 113). But most significantly Nelly in acknowledging that Heathcliff is seen to possess a 'miserable, degraded character' for which he was 'only partly responsible' identifies Heathcliff as a *pharmakon* in describing his presence as 'a moral poison that would contaminate the most virtuous' (Brontë, 1968: 124). This moral poison and contaminating threat, in its pharmaceutical function, is vital for the identification and reinforcement of the disintegrating family. As I have argued in the first chapter and elsewhere, the ideal of the family was a myth which survives by continually producing and excluding that which endangers the family, the orphan. The elimination of the orphan's threat results in the unification of the family and larger community.

Heathcliff's function is pharmaceutical: both threat and cure. However, Heathcliff is not be be assimilated into the family because of the absolute difference he embodies. The mystery that continually surrounds Heathcliff points to his unknowable nature.

> 'Is he a ghoul, or a vampire?' I mused. I had read of such hideous, incarnate demons. And then, I set myself to reflect, how I had tended him in infancy; and watched him grow to youth; and followed him almost through his whole course; and what absurd nonsense it was to yield to that sense of horror.
>
> 'But, where did he come from, the little dark thing, harboured by a good man to his bane?' muttered superstition, as I dozed into unconsciousness. And I began, half dreaming, to weary myself with imaging some fit parentage for him; and repeating my waking meditations, I tracked his existence over again, with grim varia- tions; ... as he had no surname, and we could not tell his age, we

were obliged to content ourselves with the single word,
'Heathcliff'. That came true; we were. If you enter the kirkyard,
you'll read on his headstone, only that, and the date of his death.
(Brontë, 1968: 355)

In Nelly's drifting between consciousness and unconsciousness, she
is haunted by the spectre of this Heathcliff who appears ageless, with
no known origins of lineage, no familial name. With his basilisk eyes
Heathcliff appears like a sphinx: the embodiment of silent, unknowable, impenetrable difference. This difference is the product of a
supplementary economy which interpellates him in a position of
exteriority, as a transgressive figure coming from the outside to
continually disturb the harmony of the domestic sphere. The narrative reinforces that everything about Heathcliff is unknowable. On
this level, like the supplement which embodies excess – the outsider
without origin – Heathcliff is ultimately unknowable. It is this which
allows Heathcliff both to escape originary narratives of the family and
to disturb the family narrative.

The second structuring theme present in this body of popular
orphan narratives is the association, either direct or indirect, of the
orphan figure with travelling peoples (gypsies). The nomadism which
characterises the travelling lifestyle disrupts the notion of rootedness
understood to characterise the family and the home. The legacy of
the family home functions not only as property in the family economy
but as the location of familial identity and social place; it is the place
where the history of the patrilineal family unfolds, and forms the
building block of national identity. Heathcliff, the orphan, by his very
presence continually disrupts the home and the family. Like the
cuckoo that makes its home in the nest of other birds so too
Heathcliff, by his presence and through his mysterious source of
money manages to dispossess the children of both the Earnshaw and
Linton families.

From his entrance into the family home Heathcliff is identified
as a gypsy. The 'dirty, ragged, black-haired child' who speaks some
'gibberish that nobody could understand' (Brontë, 1968: 41) has
already been identified as 'a vagabond' (Brontë, 1968: 25) whom
Hindley has marginalised through his refusal to let Heathcliff sit or

eat with the family. In fact, Hindley calls Heathcliff a 'dog', 'gipsy', a 'beggarly interloper', and an 'imp of Satan' within the space of four paragraphs (Brontë, 1968: 44). Ultimately, it is the label of gypsy that comes to identify Heathcliff: Catherine is seen to 'scour ... the country with a gipsy' (Brontë, 1968: 56); Joseph refers to Heathcliff as a 'fahl, flaysome divil of a gipsy' (Brontë, 1968: 95); and Isabella Linton, as a child, asks for Heathcliff, the 'frightful thing' to be put 'in the cellar' because, 'He's exactly like the son of the fortune-teller, that stole my tame pheasant.' (Brontë, 1968: 55). Even when Heathcliff is much older the first impression that he makes on Lockwood is that he 'forms a singular contrast to his abode and style of living. He is a dark skinned gypsy, in aspect, in dress, and manners, a gentleman' (Brontë, 1968: 7).

In fact, the identification of Heathcliff as gypsy elides into a racialised, colonised identity (cf., Perera, 1991) when he is identified as 'that strange acquisition my late neighbour made in his journey to Liverpool – a little Lascar, or an American or Spanish castaway' (Brontë, 1968: 56). The term 'Lascar' refers to an East Indian sailor or army servant. The appearance of such a racialised, colonised subject in England prefigures the later orphan figures which are considered in Chapter 5 who embody the return of the exiled, the children of emigrated orphan children and colonial subjects whose return to England pose uncomfortable problems for a British national and imperial identity. Significantly, Catherine's association with such a figure has led to her being considered as growing up in 'absolute heathenism' (Brontë, 1968: 56). It is a combination of Heathcliff's racialised difference, orphanhood, and unknown origins that leads to him being identified by Mrs Linton as both 'wicked' and 'quite unfit for a decent house' (Brontë, 1968: 56); the orphan has no place within the family economy. Indeed, Mrs Linton's objections to Heathcliff's curses serve to underline how his early 'gibberish' of a language has evolved to curses. Both, it seems, are equally offensive; both ensure that he is outside of the signifying language of family.

Even at the moment of his return, Nelly immediately identifies him through his simultaneous difference and belonging. A 'deep voice ... foreign in tone; yet ... familiar' insists that he is not a 'stranger' (Brontë, 1968: 101); the eyes were 'deep set and singular' yet they are recognised (Brontë, 1968: 102). In this moment of recognition Heathcliff displays the simultaneous sameness and unknowableness which is racialised difference.

There are other consistent representations which serve to emphasise his difference. First, he is consistently represented as a violent savage, a characterisation which differentiates him from civilised society. From early on Nelly warns him against having the look of a 'vicious cur' (Brontë, 1968: 63). His hair is described as 'a colt's mane over his eyes' (Brontë, 1968: 64). In a fit of anger he throws a tureen of hot apple sauce over the dinner guests which results in his flogging. He is constantly referred to as a 'vulgar young ruffian' and 'worse than a brute' (Brontë, 1968: 73) – depictions which cause Catherine to attempt to differentiate herself from him. Finally, although Heathcliff is treated in a way to ensure his brutalisation ('his treatment ... was enough to make a fiend of a saint'), Nelly still insists on arguing that Heathcliff was 'possessed of something diabolical ... and became daily more notable for savage sullenness and ferocity' (Brontë, 1968: 72). In fact, she intimates that Heathcliff 'contrived to convey an impression of inward and outward repulsiveness' (Brontë, 1968: 74). Lockwood revises his first impression of Heathcliff as a 'capital fellow' when Heathcliff's tone reveals 'a genuine bad nature' (Brontë, 1968: 14–5). In essence, Heathcliff comes to be constructed as the dog that he is metamorphosed into on his arrival at the Earnshaws: in his last moments with Catherine before her death he 'gnashed ... and foamed like a mad dog' causing Nelly to wonder if she were 'in the company of a creature of ... her own species' (Brontë, 1968: 176–7). After Catherine's death Heathcliff spends all his time with his dogs ('Guest are so exceedingly rare in this house that I and my dogs ... hardly know how to receive them' (Brontë, 1968: 10)). Ultimately, Heathcliff is advised to go stretch himself 'over her grave and die like a faithful dog' (Brontë, 1968: 193–4).

This difference is also continually constructed with racial/colonial overtones. Heathcliff is depicted as other, wicked, barbarous and unfit for a civilised house. In fact, in addition to being known as a 'black villain' (Brontë, 1968: 122), Heathcliff's countenance is often referred to as 'black' and he is referred to more than once in terms of a cannibal (he has 'sharp cannibal teeth' (Brontë, 1968: 193)). At many different times his behaviour is read as savage and non human: Heathcliff howls 'not like a man, but like a savage beast getting goaded to death with knives and spears' (Brontë, 1968: 183). Like other savages, Heathcliff is threatening with his cannibalistic and violent desires: Heathcliff 'kicked and trampled' Hindley and 'dashed his head repeatedly against the flags' (Brontë, 1968: 194). Heathcliff himself internalises his racial difference and the inferiority/savagery it implies; he wishes for 'light hair and a fair skin', to be 'dressed, and behaved', and to be rich as Hindley will be (Brontë, 1968: 63). Here Terry Eagleton is right about the class issues, but in his analysis misses the delineation of a civilised character also having certain racial characteristics as well as class ones. Like other colonial subjects, Heathcliff becomes identified with the land, barbarism and animality: 'Heathcliff is – an unreclaimed creature, without refinement – without cultivation; an arid wilderness of furze and whinstone ... He's not a rough diamond – a pearl-containing oyster of a rustic; he's a fierce, pitiless, wolfish man.' (Brontë, 1968: 111–12). In likening Heathcliff to a 'Titan' (Brontë, 1968: 358), Nelly is associating Heathcliff with the wild, disorderly forces of nature. This association is significant in that Heathcliff, the orphan, becomes the chaos which disturbs the harmony of the family; he as *pharmakon* is a poisonous force whose presence on the inside needs to be expelled by the forces of law and order (in the form of the family and familial genealogy) in order to effect the cure, namely that the family may be reinstated as a unified entity. The combination of racialised difference and savagery reduces Heathcliff from 'so manly' to 'diabolical' with 'basilisk eyes' and a 'ferocious sneer' (Brontë, 1968: 196), although it is rather belatedly acknowledged (but only by Nelly) that Heathcliff has 'a heart and nerves the same as ... his brother men!' (Brontë, 1968: 183). This belated acknowledgement reinforces the ambivalence that Heathcliff embodies as simultaneously difference and sameness, racialised savage and 'brother' man. It is not an incidental moment but rather something which is characteristic of his representation and that of the *pharmakon*: 'the medium in which opposites are opposed' (Derrida, 1981: 127).

However, in trying to locate *Wuthering Heights* within this specific body of popular orphan literature it is vital to recognise how *Wuthering Heights* inverts the structure of these narratives. While most of the popular orphan narratives represent travelling peoples stealing children, one could read in Mr Earnshaw's gesture of taking an 'abandoned' child (who becomes identified as a gypsy) home rather than to the authorities as an act of stealing the child – however well intentioned – from gypsies. It is also important to remember that it is this act which places Heathcliff firmly in the family seat. Thus, it is Mr Earnshaw, the familial patriarch, who imports the 'foreign' influence into his family and thus indirectly causes the destruction of his family. As discussed, Heathcliff comes to be seen as a contaminating influence, a contagion that destroys the familial ties and indirectly, all the family's members. However, this family, as with many other families represented in the novel[8] is not an ideal family, rather it is a family on the verge of disintegration. Finally, one cannot overlook the fact that the adult Heathcliff does enact the role of the gypsy in the popular orphan adventure narrative in his literal 'stealing' of the adolescent Catherine Linton and in his theft of the Earnshaw family inheritance – the land, house and social position – which rightfully belongs to Hareton whom he enslaves. In this particular narrative, Hareton's role is similar to that of Squire Hawthorn's son in *The Orphan: A Romance*: an orphan child who manages to retain an essentialised innocence in the face of the gypsy's disruption of lineage and destruction of family – like Heathcliff's. Is Heathcliff's introduction then vital to the regeneration of the family in the final union of Catherine Linton and Hareton Earnshaw?

Although Heathcliff is hated by Mrs Earnshaw the mistress, Hindley the rightful heir, and Nelly the defender of the family, he is doted on by Mr Earnshaw the patriarch who elevates him even above his own daughter Catherine. The attraction of Mr Earnshaw for Heathcliff which Nelly deems 'strange' has given rise to criticism that the tale of 'finding' Heathcliff is unconvincing and to the argument that in fact Heathcliff is Mr Earnshaw's own illegitimate child.

Whether Heathcliff is Earnshaw's illegitimate son or not, he is named after a dead son and he thus occupies, in a marginalised fashion, the place of a son to Earnshaw. The tableau in which Catherine, as a young girl, is recovering from an illness as seen by Nelly: 'Miss Cathy had been sick, and that made her still; she leant against her father's knee, and Heathcliff was lying on the floor with his head in her lap' (Brontë, 1968: 47), is of interest here. Heathcliff, with his head in Miss Cathy's lap occupies the position of lover – or even the dog into which he is initially metamorphosed. Yet he also occupies the position that Hareton/Hindley occupied before. In this moment, Heathcliff has usurped the position of the son/heir while also occupying the role of suitor. Not only will Heathcliff take the family home but it is also likely that he will take Catherine as well. It is a prescient moment in which what will come true literally is established metaphorically.

The notion that Heathcliff as lover will, if successful in his wooing, remove Catherine, through marriage, from her family home is played out in an unexpected fashion after his return. Again – like Catherine and Heathcliff's first entrance to the Linton home many year previous, we are given a Linton family tableau, but unlike the first this one is a snug, contented domestic scene and Heathcliff's entrance, via Nelly as messenger, shatters it.

> They sat together in a window whose lattice lay back against the wall, and displayed beyond the garden trees, and the wild green park, the valley of Gimmerton, with a long line of mist winding nearly to its top (for very soon after you pass the chapel, as you may have noticed, the sough that runs from the marshes joins a beck which follows the blend of the glen), Wuthering Heights rose above this silvery vapour; but our old house was invisible – it rather dips down on the other side.
>
> Both the room, and its occupants, and the scene they gazed on, looked wondrously peaceful. I shrank reluctantly from performing my errand. (Brontë, 1968: 102)

Significantly, the domestic couple is in view of both family seats; the atmosphere is harmonious. This time, unlike that when both the orphans Catherine and Heathcliff were the intruders, only Heathcliff is the outsider – Catherine has been recouped into the family. Heathcliff's entrance, via Nelly as messenger, shatters the domestic bliss. He is immediately identified by terms that inscribe a racial and class identity. 'What, the gypsy – the plough-boy?' (Brontë, 1968: 103). Catherine herself is unable to acknowledge Heathcliff's identity; the disruption of his presence is instantaneous.

Heathcliff does more than disrupt the domestic harmony; his aspiration is the severance of the bond between family and land: 'He's mine, and I want the triumph of seeing my descendant fairly lord of their estates; my child hiring their children, to till their fathers' lands for wages' (Brontë, 1968: 226). This aspiration is the culmination of a desire that first manifested itself in Heathcliff's insistence that Hindley give him his new colt to replace his own which had gone lame. Heathcliff desires that which belongs to the rightful heir and desires the annihilation of the family privilege which marginalises him. In the process he destroys the social position that the family occupied previously. 'In that manner, Hareton, who should now be the first gentleman in the neighbourhood, was reduced to a state of complete dependence on his father's inveterate enemy; and lives in his own house as a servant deprived of the advantage of wages, and quite unable to right himself, because of his friendlessness, and his ignorance that he has been wronged' (Brontë, 1968: 205).

Such destruction is not merely the reappropriation of land in Marxist terms as Eagleton has argued in *Myths of Power* (Eagleton, 1988), but is a process by which Heathcliff's disruption of the family results in the production of orphans/the reproduction of his own orphan state. Hareton is indirectly rendered an orphan and deprived of his familial inheritance by Heathcliff's actions. It is an act of deprivation which is reproduced with young Catherine from the moment of her birth. It is Heathcliff's reappearance that results indirectly in Catherine's illness and subsequent death. Heathcliff's imprisonment of young Catherine contributes to Edgar's death and thus finishes off the orphaning process that his actions had initiated at the birth of this 'feeble orphan' and 'unwelcomed infant' whose 'beginning was as friendless as its end is likely to be' (Brontë, 1968: 180).

So, Heathcliff's role in the family narrative as orphan is a *pharmakon*, a contaminating and disruptive presence. It is a role in which he is seen to exult: 'Now my bonny lad you are mine! And we'll see if one tree won't grow as crooked as another, with the same wind to twist it!' (Brontë, 1968: 204). Heathcliff takes a pleasure in his enslavement of Hareton/erasure of the family memory and history in Hareton:

> He has satisfied my expectations – If he were born a fool I should not enjoy it half so much – But he's no fool; and I can sympathise with all his feelings, having felt them myself – I know what he suffers now, for instance, exactly – it is merely a beginning of what he shall suffer, though. And he'll never be able to emerge from his bathos of coarseness, and ignorance. I've got him faster than his scoundrel of a father secured me, and lower; for he takes a pride in his brutishness. (Brontë, 1968: 237)

In fact, Heathcliff delights in the suffering of his own offspring as well. For instance he does not demonstrate any parental affection for his son. Instead he says of Linton: 'None here care what becomes of him; if you do, act the nurse; if you do not, lock him up and leave him' (Brontë, 1968: 315). Thus, Heathcliff's destruction of the family is applied equally to his own family as to the Lintons and the Earnshaws. Heathcliff tells Linton that his mother, Heathcliff's wife, is 'a wicked slut' (Brontë, 1968: 226); Heathcliff treats his dying child 'tyrannically and wickedly' (Brontë, 1968: 279). In fact, although Heathcliff is the first to accuse Hindley of having destroyed his family, 'He hates you [Hindley] – they all hate you – that's the truth! A happy family you have! And a pretty state you're come to!', the fact is that Heathcliff's own family relationships have completely broken down: 'You're worse than a heathen – treating your own flesh and blood in that manner!' (Brontë, 1968: 83).

In the end, the responsibility for the preservation of the family lineage falls to the unlikely figure of Joseph. Joseph's efforts ensure that Hareton is instilled with 'a pride of name, and of his lineage' (Brontë, 1968: 215). Thus, when the familial order is restored at the end of the novel, it is ensured that the same familial traditions are reinstated. But the power Heathcliff represents ensures that there are no overt moves to destroy him,[9] rather the family must wait for his self-destruction. Ultimately, then, through the figure of Joseph, law and order restore themselves. The family does not destroy itself, but the familial lineage is triumphant over the foreign disorder and lack of genealogy that the orphan Heathcliff represents.

The third structuring representation of the popular orphan adventure narratives, the criminalisation of the orphan figure either by discursive association or through necessity, has only minor significance in *Wuthering Heights*. When the orphans Heathcliff and Catherine first trespass on the Linton property it is Heathcliff who is described as an 'out-and-outer' and a 'foul-mouthed thief' (Brontë, 1968: 55). When they discover Heathcliff is but a boy they still prophesy that 'the villain scowls so plainly in his face, would it not be a kindness to the country to hang him at once, before he shows his nature in acts, as well as features?' (Brontë, 1968: 55). On his return the speculations about the source of his money include wondering if he made 'a fortune more promptly, on the English highways' (Brontë, 1968: 99–100). Despite his well-to-do appearance on his return he is still identified as a 'low ruffian' (Brontë, 1968: 124).

Although Heathcliff is recuperated into the family his experience is predominately that of being marginalised, outcast. On his return, Hindley's first actions are to drive Heathcliff 'to the servants', to deprive Heathcliff 'of the instructions of the curate', and to insist that Heathcliff 'should labour out of doors instead' (Brontë, 1968: 51). When Catherine spends her first spell at the Lintons, Heathcliff becomes 'ten times' more 'careless and uncared for' (Brontë, 1968: 59). On her return Catherine comments on how 'dirty' Heathcliff is (Brontë, 1968: 60); the Lintons only agree to allow their children to visit Wuthering Heights on the condition that the 'naughty swearing boy' Heathcliff is kept separate (Brontë, 1968: 60). Although Heathcliff tries to conform ('Nelly, make me decent, I'm going to be good' (Brontë, 1968: 62)), he is unable to assimilate into the family. The same is true on his return when to all intents and purposes Heathcliff has been transformed by a possible stint in the army – suggested by his 'upright carriage' (Brontë, 1968: 104–5) – the social organisation in combination with the navy which often became a source of employment for orphans. Although it is stated that Heathcliff is 'reformed in every respect, apparently – quite a Christian – offering the right hand of fellowship to his enemies all round!' (Brontë, 1968: 108), Nelly still insists that she can detect 'A half-civilized ferocity ... in the depressed brows, and eyes full of black fire, but it was subdued' in a face that is characterised by its intelligence (Brontë, 1968: 104–5). Thus, Heathcliff remains marginalised in society because of his unknown origins – in terms of his lack of a familial name and therefore inherited social position. When Isabella considers marrying Heathcliff she is reminded of the 'degradation of an alliance with a nameless man'; Linton also worries that his own property 'in default of heirs male' might pass to Heathcliff (Brontë, 1968: 109–10). When considering both these issues, Linton, like Nelly, comes to the conclusion that although Heathcliff's 'exterior was altered, his mind was unchangeable, and unchanged' (Brontë, 1968: 109–10).

Although the focus of this particular chapter is on the representation of the male orphan figure within popular orphan narratives, it is important to acknowledge that Catherine too is an orphan – although her orphanhood differs from Heathcliff's because of her known lineage, familial name and home. For that matter, Hindley, Hareton and eventually Catherine Linton are all orphans as well. What I do want to consider briefly is how Catherine's orphanhood is further complicated by her gender.

When describing her own marriage, Catherine demonstrates how gender can pose problems for the rootedness and indigenous kinship of which Eliot writes. Catherine tells of her experience as a woman being that of an outcast: 'I have been wrenched from the Heights, and every early association, and my all in all, as Heathcliff was at that time, and been converted, at a stroke into Mrs Linton, the lady of Thrushcross Grange, and the wife of a stranger; an exile, and outcast, thenceforth, from what had been my world' (Brontë, 1968: 137). Catherine's marriage, and her subsequent removal from her family home, give her a discursive status similar to that of Heathcliff, namely an exile and outcast. In particular, Catherine talks of her moving to her new marital home in terms of being uprooted.

Marriage for Catherine translates into leaving her rooted home, the familiar sights, sounds and acquaintances. Marriage is constructed as a conversion, in terms of belief, name and symbolic rebirth. Thus, leaving home through marriage works in the narrative as an orphaning process – or in Catherine's case a double orphaning process.

Ironically, Catherine undertakes what can be read as a self-orphaning process in order to provide for Heathcliff, the orphan; as a woman Catherine has no other ability but to gain power through marriage. When Nelly accuses her of deserting Heathcliff, Catherine makes clear that if she married Heathcliff they would be beggars but 'if I marry Linton, I can aid Heathcliff to rise, and place him out of my brother's power' (Brontë, 1968: 90). This passage leads to one of the most famous passages of the book.

> If all else perished, and he remained, and he were annihilated, the Universe would turn to a mighty stranger. I should not seem a part of it. My love for Linton is like the foliage in the woods. Time will change it, I'm well aware, as winter changes the trees – my love for Heathcliff resembles the eternal rocks beneath – a source of little visible delight, but necessary. Nelly, I am Heathcliff – he's always, always in my mind – not as a pleasure, any more than I am always a pleasure to myself – but, as my own being – so, don't talk of our separation again – it is impracticable. (Brontë, 1968: 90)

When Catherine says that she is Heathcliff she is embracing her loss of self as an orphan. Yet simultaneously, as a representative of the family, Catherine's identification with Heathcliff is an act of naming the difference contained within; it is the moment when the family is explicitly shown to contain the orphan within. The necessity of Heathcliff's presence/identity for Catherine as well as hers for him represents how profoundly intertwined the family and orphan are.

In a novel which emphasises marks of difference, Catherine's fiery temperament gives her a kinship with Heathcliff. In fact she argues that Heathcliff is more herself than she is or at the very least, 'Whatever our souls are made of, his and mine are the same' (Brontë, 1968: 89). Catherine and Heathcliff also share a kinship of desire and of violence. After all there is no mistaking the 'tingling' in her fingers as she first slapped Nelly on the cheek with 'a stinging blow that filled both eyes with water' then shook Hareton 'till the poor child waxed livid' and then 'cuffed Edgar in a way that could not be mistaken for jest' (Brontë, 1968: 78). However, Catherine's orphanhood is different from Heathcliff's. As Catherine comes from an established family and therefore has a known genealogy she can be easily assimilated into the social family; it does not take very long before the 'wild, hatless little savage' is changed into 'a very dignified person with brown ringlets falling from the cover of a feathered beaver' (Brontë, 1968: 58).

Catherine shares the same exile as Heathcliff; both regard Heaven not as a final reward but a land of exile if the other is not there. In her dream, 'Heaven did not seem to be my home; and I broke my heart with weeping to come back to earth; and the angels were so angry that they flung me out, into the middle of the heath on the top of Wuthering Heights; where I woke sobbing for joy' (Brontë, 1968: 88). Heathcliff on the other hand comes to the conclusion that 'Heaven would be a land of exile to ... [Catherine], unless, with her mortal body, she cast away her mortal character also' (Brontë, 1968: 175). Thus, Catherine's orphanhood, unlike Heathcliff's, is one which can be reassimilated into the family but ultimately one which continues to constrain her because of her gender.

In conclusion, Heathcliff embodies the difference within which plays a pharmaceutical function disrupting yet ultimately reinforcing notions of family and nation. Throughout Heathcliff remains unknowable and unassimilable: a racialised foreign figure with no known origins who attempts to dispossess the indigenous families. In offering Heathcliff a number of possible narratives from 'a regular black' to 'a prince in disguise', with a father who is an Emperor of China and mother an Indian queen, who was kidnapped by 'wicked sailors' and sold into slavery (Brontë, 1968: 63–4), Nelly taps into the popular imperial narratives which revolve around orphan sailors and barbarous pirates. But this will be the subject of the next chapter. Paradoxically, it is through Heathcliff's son and Catherine's daughter that the difference is excluded and the indigenous families are regenerated, yet the presence of Heathcliff's son ensures that the difference remains within.

3

Popular orphan adventure narratives

THE CONSIDERATION of the unassimilable figure of
Heathcliff does raise another issue: what happens to the
orphan children of the poor who are not ultimately
recouped into families? This marginalised figure without family ties
dominates juvenile literature, specifically popular orphan adventure
narratives – the legacy of which is to be found in *The Pirates of
Penzance* written in 1879. In this literature, the orphan becomes the
sailor who, in finding employment on the seas in either the merchant
navy or marines, does the work of empire. Whether working in the
imperial economy or defending the empire on the high seas battling
foreign enemies and pirates, the orphan sailor is crucial to the
defence of the empire, the centre of which, ironically, is the very
Victorian family structure in which he could not find a place. This
section will examine a representative sample of such imperial juvenile literature in order to explore the role of the orphan in imperial
endeavours.

Imperial juvenile literature not only worked to consolidate 'the
energising myth of empire' (Green, 1980: XI) across classes
(Mackenzie, 1986: 4) but also helped to propagate the Arnoldian
values of the public-school namely, 'ancient patriotism', 'heroic self-
sacrifice', 'passionate devotion', 'pride of patriotism', 'fortitude,
self-reliance, intrepidity', 'public spirit' and so on (Bratton, 1986:
74–5). Such values rely on an implicit notion of civilisation; they were
offered as the foundation of an imperial England. Although the
public-school nature of these values meant that they were most likely
to be espoused by the classes which sent their children to public

schools they did have a wider currency in the society at large. Imperialism may have been seen as a civilising mission by both the middle classes, who were economically benefiting from empire, and the religious missionaries eager to proselytise to the 'heathens', but the work of policing empire offered employment to the very poor and the working classes – particularly orphan boys. The orphan adventure narratives that represent this particular experience offer particular insight, not into the glamour and exotic adventure often portrayed in literature representing middle-class boys, but into the cruelty and brutality of both the endeavour and the treatment received by the orphan while on the ship.

Victorian society's use of the orphan to represent a marginalised 'otherness' and difference within replicates the same workings of the very colonial discourse and power used against its external 'Others' in the form of colonial subjects of foreign threats to imperial supremacy. It is a powerful discourse which not only constructs notions of civilisation and savagery but also reinforces them. One area where this discourse is easily identifiable at work is in early Victorian orphan adventure narratives. Significantly, one of the very figures who suffers most from the workings of this within Victorian England – the orphan children of the poor – becomes a key player in the imperial efforts to reinforce empire outside of England. The orphan adventure narrative which best embodies this paradox is Charles Dickens' and Wilkie Collins's short story, co-written as a Christmas story in 1857, 'The Perils of Certain English Prisoners, and Their Treasure in Women, Children, Silver and Jewels' (*Perils*).[10] In this story the protagonist is Gill Harker, a working-class orphan who joins the Royal Marines. The story opens with Gill and the other marines on duty, in what Dickens refers to as South America (Central America), protecting the English colony and the silver mine they were working. The colony comes under attack by pirates after having been betrayed by one of the native workers, Christian George King. During the ensuing battle, Gill distinguishes himself by his brave actions and ultimately helps the survivors to escape from the pirates. Gill's bravery is rewarded and he returns to England, somewhat unwillingly, to live with Captain Carton and his wife. It is Mrs Carton, the woman Gill loves, who records his story as Gill is illiterate.

Perils is a story to which both Patrick Brantlinger in *Rule of Darkness: British Literature and Imperialism, 1830–1914* and Robert Young in *Colonial Desire: Hybridity in Theory, Culture and Race* refer fleetingly as an example of the inscription of colonial discourse within Victorian culture and the intervention made by literary figures into the politics of imperialism. I offer a reading of Dickens's *Perils* that locates it within the body of popular orphan adventure narratives which work to reinforce imperial endeavours. Initially, use of the orphan figure is highlighted as colonial agent in popular fiction at the time. In the second part, *Perils* is located within a wider cultural context, namely Victorian attitudes to empire in response to the Cawnpore mutiny.

In August and September 1857 the *Illustrated London News* (*ILN*) ran a substantial coverage of the mutinies in India in the form of editorials, articles, reports of parliamentary debates and what I term 'survivor' letters. These 'survivor' letters, with which Dickens was familiar, were eyewitness accounts, often by soldiers, of individual experiences of the mutiny. Elsewhere, I suggest that the pattern of events, betrayal and duplicity revealed in these 'survivor' letters can be seen partly to structure *Perils* which is written as a personal account of a Royal Marine's, Gill's, survival of mutiny in South America (Peters, 2000). The linkage between the media coverage and *Perils* is very persuasive, but so too is the linkage between *Perils* and a large body of imperial fictional tales which can be called popular orphan adventure narratives. This chapter explores the positioning of *Perils* in this type of literature.

The intertextuality between *Perils* and the survivor letters signals itself, but *Perils* also displays a revealing excess which far surpasses these survivor letters. I will give one brief example. On 12 September 1857 the *ILN* ran a letter that it claims to have received from a British soldier in Allahabad on 20 June 1857 who survived what he describes as the attack by 'a thousand infuriate fiends ... [and convicts who were] excited by opium and drink'. In *Perils* the depiction is of 'the barbarous Pirates, scum of all nations, headed by such men as the hideous little Portuguese monkey, and the one-eyed English convict ... The worst men in the world picked out from the worst, to do the cruellest and most atrocious deeds that ever stained it? The howling, murdering, black-flag waving, mad, and drunken crowds of devils that had overcome use by numbers and by treachery?' (Dickens, 1857: 66). Crucially included in the motley crew of pirates is the one-eyed English convict – a figure who represents more than the reworking of the stories told to Dickens when he was a child. It is the representation of the fear of the possibility that the criminalised population, thought to be safely transported, will not only escape to threaten colonial outposts, but on their return will destabilise the heart of empire.

Later, in the figure of Magwitch and his return to claim 'Look'ee here Pip, I am your father' it is possible to identify that the parent of the orphan Pip is not Joe or even the state but the transported convict whose return is not only literal but embodied in the figure of Pip – a figure created by Magwitch's money. The excess of the accounts in *Perils* compared to the survivor letters alerts one not only to the fear of the other embedded within colonial desire but also to the imaginative response to the threatening nature of empire. Adopting a formulaic structure in this response would allow a clear identification and destruction of the threatening enemy and a reaffirmation of national and masculine myths.

Popular orphan adventure narratives provide one such forum for such imaginative responses to empire. These narratives are not dissimilar to the working-class soldier narratives, which Carolyn Steedman considers in *The Radical Soldier's Tale*, in their presentation of 'a drama of alienation, journeying and arrival' (Steedman, 1988: 37). Popular orphan narratives are characterised by the suffering and struggle undergone by a central figure who is usually alienated, as an orphan, from the social structures and institutions which are organised around the concept of the family. The tales, in their representation of the orphan figure, often espousing the very public school values Bratton identifies, are critical of the social family's failure of responsibility to its orphans. The heroism of the orphan is to be found in his endurance and retention of an inherent innocence despite the deprivation and ill-treatment suffered. On one level, these popular orphan adventure narratives tell of internal colonisation and a profound otherness within Victorian society. The orphan occupies the place of the colonised subject within Victorian society: dispossessed, without rights, and embodying a difference to be excluded. On another level, the orphan's lack of rootedness and obvious social obligations identifies him as a possible agent of empire.

In using the orphan to represent otherness and difference, Victorian society reproduces the workings of colonial discourse. Popular orphan adventure narratives, such as Peter Buchan's *The Orphan Sailor: A Tragic Tale of Love, of Pity, and of Woe* (1834), construct discourses of civilisation, patriotism and imperialism. In doing so these narratives represent, and justify, imperialism as a patriotic impulse in order to mask the nature of its capitalist imperatives. The male orphan figure is a popular device in narratives that not only explore social power structures and imperial ideology but which also encode notions of savagery. Popular orphan adventure tales, like *The Orphan Sailor*, are deeply masculinist in their emphasis on the militaristic hierarchical structure of the ship with its all-male sailors; the masculine nature of these tales in turn reflects the gendered representation of the patriotic impulse and the imperial endeavour. In *The Orphan Sailor*, the historical specificity is that of the Mediterranean under the control and hegemony of Barbary's piracy: Algeria. By orientalising the Algerians as a despotic foreign threat to the English, the tale works to justify the English imperial impulse as a civilising one: disciplined English soldiers confronting barbarous pirates. In *The Orphan Sailor* the orphan is victimised within society, represented by the ship, and actually enslaved, taken prisoner by Algerian pirates and sold as a slave in Algiers. This literal enslavement can be read as representative of a parallel discursive enslavement that the orphan experiences on the ship and formerly in England – a comment on the nature of the centre of the British Empire. Throughout both the victimisation and the enslavement the orphan William is able to display inherent qualities such as bravery, daring and resourcefulness. However, the tale works as a melodramatic tragedy to represent the orphan as ultimately pathetic – one who is doomed to a life of tragedy regardless of his endeavours: after William escapes and is reunited with his true love, Jessie, she is killed during their voyage in another shipwreck and William is discursively returned to his original state outside the family as an orphan 'friendless and forlorn'. The narrative of self-help then does not translate into class mobility. In *The Orphan Sailor's* use of the victimised, but brave, male orphan to defend the nation's interests from barbarous pirates, and the inability of this same nation to reward the hero, one can easily identify the structure of *Perils*.

On another level, orphan adventure narratives also work to mythologise a bourgeois domesticity. Suffice to say at this moment, many of these narratives represent a return to a pastoral existence as a new narrative of domesticity in order to obfuscate the pressing urban problems that confronted them. The imaginative valuing of the rural as a site for domesticity also underlines the perception of empire. It is the impulse to widen the boundaries of home through imperial endeavours and to cultivate the wilderness into a domestic garden discussed earlier (Dawson, 1994: 65). Popular orphan adventure narratives play a part in this reforming impulse which addresses problems, in the form of orphans and colonial subjects, facing the achievement of this ideal, both at home and abroad. In this way, orphan adventure narratives come close to the soldier tales that Graham Dawson considers in which 'Melodrama ... [with] its strong moral contrasts and heightened intensity of response produce a specific kind of idealised adventure hero' (Dawson, 1994: 112). Charles Wall's *The Orphan's Isle* (1838) is an excellent example of such a pastoral retreat and displays a differing class focus from that of *The Orphan Sailor*. In the latter, the main character William is obviously of the impoverished, migrant street population whereas *The Orphan's Isle*, written as an autobiographical fragment, portrays children identified as middle class by their family upbringing and their education. In this narrative the orphans receive instruction, rather than enslavement, from the indigenous population. It is significant that this instruction occurs in the rural periphery away from the urban metropolis: it can be read as an attempt to recover both the rural and the family in the domestic.

Elements of both *The Orphan Sailor* and *The Orphan's Isle*, combined with the discourse of self-help are easily identifiable in Lady Isabella Stoddart's (pseudonym Martha Blackford) *The Orphan of Waterloo* (1840) which is concerned with issues of family, domesticity, class and imperialism both within and outside of England. In *The Orphan Sailor*, the ship not only transmits imperialism's agents but also simultaneously acts as the microcosm of society, reflecting social structures and re-enacting current social debates. In *The Orphan of Waterloo*, the demonised foreigner, Napoleon, is vanquished by the morally superior English, but this historical specificity – like that of Algeria – serves as an orientalised backdrop to celebrate successful English military exploits and, in their defeat of Napoleon, encode their superiority in the narrative. *The Orphan of Waterloo* locates the class narrative in one of the military families in which the adopted orphan Hubert, who embodies self-help, is relied on to save the degenerate, quasi-aristocratic middle class. In *Perils* Gill saves the very people in the colony that he resents seeing as 'good livers', people who have had an easy life while his own has been so difficult.

In *Perils* then, it is possible to identify Dickens combining the orphan narrative of internal colonisation (in the face of domesticity and the family narrative – as seen in *The Orphan; A Romance* by Mootoo discussed in Chapter 2) with the imperial orphan adventure narratives (where the orphan unwittingly acts as colonial agent, confronting pirates and 'barbarians' in the defence of the empire and domesticity). *Perils* offers a multi-layered comment in its critique of English society and in its sympathy with empire. I now explore the tale in more detail, in order to identify its borrowings from orphan adventure narratives and to probe the issues of agency and ambivalence that characterise the orphan hero. In order to do this I consider first the imperial function of this type of narrative, and Dickens's role in the imperial arena, by exploring Victorian attitudes to empire in response to the Cawnpore mutiny. Then I look at *Perils* itself as a vehicle for imperialism. Finally, I look at *Perils* as a critique of English society from the margins.

Victorian attitudes to empire in response to the Cawnpore mutiny

In the midst of the media coverage of the mutiny the article 'A Very Black Act' appears in *Household Words* on 26 September 1857; it was an article written by the British editor of an Indian provincial newspaper on the newly introduced censorship of newspapers in India which were seen as potentially subversive publications. In a revealing passage this editor saw his role as now including 'the duties of armed volunteer, policeman, special messenger, and anything else required by the state at this critical juncture' (Anon., 1857: 293). This piece reveals that the press was not only an arm of empire in India but was directly involved in the policing of empire. One can only wonder what parallels Dickens drew between the imperial role of the editor in India and the editor in Britain.

Dickens did consciously enter the colonial arena through his popular fiction and short stories. On 1 October 1853 Dickens wrote: 'A nation without fancy, with some romance, never did, never can, never will, hold a great place under the sun' (Dickens, 1853). For Dickens, imaginative stories and cultural products are not only rejuvenating influences but can be seen to contribute to national greatness. More specifically, in *Perils* Dickens's emphasis on the marine soldiers' (particularly Gill's and Harry's), selfless heroism and devotion to a British society which has mistreated them is part of Dickens's self-proclaimed project to celebrate 'without any vulgar catchpenny connection or application, some of the best qualities of the English character that have been shown in India' (Dickens, 1937–38: 2; 889). This celebration of the best qualities of the English character in India serves as a pointed commentary to editorials which were running in *ILN* and widespread public criticism of the British rule in India: Sir Charles Napier's memoirs of his service in India had just been published and were highly critical of this rule. On a personal level, Dickens would want to believe in the best qualities of the English in India – or in other colonies for that matter – because in July 1857 he sent his sixteen-year-old son Walter off to India as a soldier in the 26th Native Infantry.

But a common concern Dickens did share was that the mutiny could spread throughout the empire. This concern was expressed most succinctly in an editorial of the *ILN* of 1 August 1857 as the news of the extent of the uprising reached England. The editorial argues that 'Every day that Delhi remains in the hands of the mutineers is a day of peril to British power. Its possession ... is an incentive to rebellion ... to chiefs and potentates who remain faithful from fear and not from love' (110). The possible loss of empire had economic and political ramifications and threatened national mythology. It was feared that with the 'empire in the East ... imperilled', British 'prestige' and 'supremacy' among the European nations was also at risk (*Lloyd's Weekly*, 6 September 1857: 6). It is possible then to read, as Patrick Brantlinger does, Dickens's location of the tale in Central America (and what Dickens refers to as the West Indies), as an extension of the idea of mutiny to other parts of empire by equating East Indians, native Indians and Africans with each other and therefore implying that all 'natives' are untrustworthy (Brantlinger, 1988: 207). Dickens's underlying comment can be identified in the protagonist Gill's warning to 'trust no Sambo, and, above all, if he could get any good chance at Christian George King [CGK], not to lose it, but to put him out of the world' (Dickens, 1987: 184).

This hard-line advocacy of a brutal putting down of mutiny echoes the agitation within the media to rule through fear as found in an *ILN* editorial of 22 August 1857 which argues that 'The spectacle of power is that which we should exhibit ... Asiatics differ not simply in religion, but in blood, from Europeans. They worship Power. They understand the strong arm, the inflexible will, the unrelenting determination' (186). (In *Perils* Gill is characterised by the Maltese leader of the mutiny as 'determined'.) In this context of the desire to rule through the spectacle of power, there was also a rabid media coverage which in September 1857 claimed that, 'Children have been compelled to eat the quivering flesh of their murdered parents, after which they were literally torn asunder by the laughing fiends who surrounded them' (*The Times*, 17 September 1857) and that 'Parents ... were made to swallow portions of the flesh cut from the limbs of the children, and afterwards burnt over a slow fire' (Dawson, 1994; 87). These reports, which were on the most part unsubstantiated rumour arising from the British community within India itself, caused a collective cry for revenge from the general population in England. Thomas Macaulay described 'an account of that dreadful military execution at Peshawar – forty men blown all at once from the mouths of cannon, their heads, legs, arms flying in all directions – ... as being read with delight by people who three weeks ago were against capital punishment' (Hutchins, 1967; 85). Graham Dawson highlights the response in the media as predominately a call for 'vengeance upon the fiends' and for 'the extermination and rooting out from the face of the earth the Mohammedan and Brahminised demons who have committed crimes on British women and maidens too horrible to name'. Even the radical *Newcastle Chronicle* advocated 'vengeance ... sharp and bloody, ... [They should be] exterminated as if they were so many wild beasts'(Dawson, 1994: 87).

In the 'exterminate and root out' rhetoric it is possible to recognise echoes in Dickens's infamous letter of 4 October 1857 to Angela Burdett-Coutts in which he takes the strong-arm, inflexible will discourse ('trust no Sambo ... [but] put him out of the world') to its logical, 'proto-fascist' (Tambling, 1995; 189) conclusion: Dickens's answer to mutiny is genocide.

> I wish I were Commander in Chief in India. The first thing I would do to strike that Oriental race ... should be to proclaim to them, in their language, that I considered my holding that appointment by the leave of God, to mean that I should do my utmost to exterminate the Race upon whom the stain of the late cruelties rested; ... I was there for that purpose and no other, and was now proceeding, with ... merciful swiftness of execution, to blot it out of mankind and raze it off the face of the Earth.
>
> My love to Mrs Brown, with these sentiments. (Dickens, 1937–8; 350–1)

It is during these cries for vengeance that *Perils* was written.

Perils as an imperial tale

As with *The Orphan Sailor*, *The Orphan's Isle* and *The Orphan of Waterloo*, *Perils* is concerned with issues of family, extension of domesticity, imperialism and a colonial discourse of savagery versus civilisation applied both to England and to colonial subjects. *Perils* revolves around Gill, a male orphan figure who, defined as outside the family, has suffered the oppressed existence of the marginalised: the social institutions have failed him in their parental role. Gill's literal orphanhood is also a metaphoric orphanhood which manifests itself not only in the form of self-exile, but in an illiteracy which blocks his entry into a system of language and discourse which might have afforded him an identity. Gill's narration of this tale is both an attempt to place himself within a discourse and simultaneously the final act of agency on the part of the discourse which marginalises him firmly in the space of outsider.

Victorian cultural and colonial discourses intersect when Gill functions in the imperial arena where his experience of ill-treatment is applied to others throughout the world: Gill's endeavours to flee his own ill-treatment in England have resulted in him joining the Royal Marines. Thus, Gill now acts as colonial agent who not only works to maintain and to police the colonial frontier, but who, through his participation, helps to reproduce the ill-treatment of colonial subjects. Thus, as with other popular orphan adventure narratives, the use of the male orphan figure explores notions of savagery and otherness embedded within colonial discourse and manifested in the form of indigenous people and barbarous pirates. Significantly, as colonial agent, Gill also perpetuates this discourse in his consciously held racist and colonial attitudes. He claims that 'I never did like Natives, except in the form of oysters' (Dickens, 1987: 170).

What is more disturbing however is Gill's embodiment of racist irrational hatred and a strong desire to do violence to these 'native Sambos, [named as such] when they are half-negro and half-Indian' (Dickens, 1987: 166). This is evident when he first meets Christian George King (CGK) of whom he says, 'I should have kicked Christian

George King – who was no more a Christian than he was a King or a George – over the side, without exactly knowing why, except that it was the right thing to do' (Dickens, 1987: 166).

In his immediate hatred and distrust of CGK, Gill functions on at least three levels: first, on the narrative level of melodrama, he helps to establish CGK as the villain of the piece; second, Gill can be read as reproducing, and being in the position to reproduce, the ill-treatment that he suffered both within Victorian England and through its agents around the empire; and third, Gill embodies an intense racism which desires to destroy the object of hatred – the racialised other.

However, the class structure embedded within the narrative means that Gill *shares* the margins, albeit unequally and with some discomfort, with CGK. This discomfort manifests itself in his haunting by CGK. The latter, as if part of Gill's subconscious, appears in a dream vision 'flitting ... dancing ... and peeping' (Dickens, 1987: 176). The dream melts into reality as Gill awakes and CGK is there as if conjured up. The haunting vision forms the basis not only for Gill's unrecognised premonition but also his discovery of the full knowledge of the treachery involved.

In the binary relationship between Gill and CGK, it is possible to identify the colonial mirror image of the coloniser in the other. A crucial part of the colonial mirror process that Bhabha writes about is the element of mimicry and the overt irony involved in this (Bhabha, 1984: 125–33). In the representation of CGK – which anticipates Conrad's 'dog in a parody of breeches' statement about Marlow's African assistant in *Heart of Darkness* (and with whom Achebe rightly took issue) – Dickens adds the dimension of what could now be called mimicry in CGK's doubling of Gill. The 'Sambo vagabond' is 'berry sorry' and claims to 'cry, English fashion!'. Gill describes his English fashion of crying as 'to screw his black knuckles into his eyes, howl like a dog, and role himself on his back on the sand. It was trying not to kick him' (Dickens, 1987: 171). But on another level, Gill finds a distorted image of the colonial indigenous population in CGK. It is in the portrait of Christian George King that Dickens is at his most objectionable. Not content with describing his movements as spasmodic and unnatural (as if he has not evolved into flowing motions), he has CGK nodding 'as if it was jerked out of him by a most violent hiccup – which is the way with those savages' and his speech is a 'very objectionable kind of convulsions'. Ultimately, Dickens animalises CGK: he runs at 'a wolf's trot'; he is 'barbarous' or 'barbarian' (which reminds one of the Barbary Coast and pirates of *The Orphan Sailor*); he 'cluck[s]'; he speaks in a 'low croak'; and he clings to Gill's leg in battle like a 'serpent'. The final image is not only of 'a Traitor and a Spy' but also of an 'animal … [who is] shot through the heart … [and covered with] slime' (Dickens, 1987: 170–205).

This clucking and croaking bears a strong resemblance to Dickens's non-fictional writing on 'the noble savage':

> I have not the least belief in the Noble Savage. I consider him a prodigious nuisance, and an enormous superstition. His calling rum firewater, and me a pale face, wholly fail to reconcile me to him. I don't care what he calls me. I call him a savage, and I call a savage a something to be civilised off the face of the earth. I think a mere gent (which I take to be the lowest form of civilisation) better than a howling, whistling, clucking, stamping, jumping, tearing savage … in the course of this world's development, … his absence is a blessed relief and an indispensable preparation for the sowing of the very first seeds of … humanity. (Dickens, 1987: 467)

It is not a coincidence then that Gill is the first to uncover the treachery, 'I had seen it all, in a moment … that Christian George King was a double-dyed traitor and a most infernal villain' (Dickens, 1987: 182). Within the larger cultural context, *Perils* here reaffirms national and masculine myths as embodied in the virtues of the public school. It is a moment which highlights Dickens's own imperial project. Gill, unlike the soldier from Allahabad in the survivor letter published in the *ILN* that I opened with, is woken by a dream vision and an inner knowledge rather than a direct attack: therefore he is not caught napping but discovers the treachery through alertness and a good soldier's instinct. Gill, in contrast to the same soldier from Allahabad, does not flee the fighting or the attack but stays to defend the women and children in the fort; he displays a valour and determination that is greatly acclaimed. It can be read as an endeavour to undo, or to rewrite, the inability to British soldiers to protect their women and children in India. Thus, it is possible to identify Dickens overtly stoking the fires of empire, in a format best known for its celebration of English military success, in an attempt to reconcile inner discontents (and perhaps his own discontentment) with the imperial project.

In Gill's attitudes and admission of a desire to kick CGK, he can be seen in the role of oppressor or slave-master. The slave-master connection is made explicit in the final dark and menacing exhibition of CGK which evokes the spectacle of lynching: 'He was left hanging to the tree, all alone, with the red sun making a kind of a dead sunset on his black face' (Dickens, 1987: 205–6). It is an image which Dickens has used before with the 'lynching' of Bill Sykes in *Oliver Twist*. The idyllic paradise has been purged of its demon enabling the colonisers to revel in the Garden of Eden, the restored garden of domesticity, and the sailors claim a spiritual reward: 'We went out of the gate too, marching along the level plain towards the serene blue sky, as if we were marching straight to Heaven' (Dickens, 1987: 207).

However, the tale is a complex orphan adventure narrative which does not only work on a simple Manichean level. In a movement from the colony back Home, it is also an adventure narrative which revolves around the domestic ideal and its class location. As an orphan Gill is alienated from England, English society and its manifestation in the colony. He compares his 'hard life' with 'the life of the English on the Island [which] seemed too easy and too gay to please [him]. Gill finds it 'hard' that the English on the island should have 'all the halfpence' while he has 'all the kicks' (Dickens, 1987: 167). As with *The Orphan of Waterloo*, the colony relies on the valour and resourcefulness of Gill, the orphan, to rescue them.

The reflection of English society and domesticity in the colonial mirror transforms it into a hybrid place as it mixes with the South American coast. It is represented as 'a pretty place ... partly South American and partly English'; 'like a bit of home that had got chipped off and had floated away to that spot, accommodating itself to circumstances as it drifted along' (Dickens, 1987: 167–8). This may look an endearing hybrid, but the colonial mapping of space should not be overlooked. The colony may fly both the Union Jack and the South American flag on the same pole, but the space is segregated with the Sambos' huts on the beach, the English within the compound and an encounter space where all could come together (Dickens, 1987: 168). Despite the fact that Dickens adds this last detail to portray a happy colony, the reality is (as mentioned already) that the indigenous are not counted as part of the colony in any way. Yet, the notion of chipping off and floating away is an act of breaking from, and perhaps an act of mutiny towards, England which foreshadows Gill's final feelings.

With the familial configuration that is developed in the domestic narrative it is not difficult to see why Gill strongly resents the life and the colony. During his time in the colony Gill regresses to childhood, which returns him to the state during which he was subjected to internal colonisation: '[I] fell asleep with wet eyelashes, and a sore, sore heart. Just as I had done when I was a child, and had been worse used than usual ... I laid myself down on my face on the beach, and cried for the first time since I had frightened birds as a boy at Snorridge Bottom, to think what a poor, ignorant, low-placed, private soldier I was' (Dickens, 1987: 181).

Ultimately, the paradox of the ending necessitates that Gill be reconciled to symbols of British colonial authority while remaining alienated from, and hostile to, British internal social structures. This is so because Dickens needs to validate the colonial power structure as proper and civilised in response to the Cawnpore mutiny, while maintaining his long held criticism of English society (most succinctly displayed in the portraits of the self-important Pordages). Thus, in a splitting of his psyche, Gill becomes admiring of his military superiors and recognises his resentment as misplaced.[11] Gill compensates for his lack of family by finding a new domesticity (familial) in the Navy.

During his escape from the pirates Gill recognises his alienation from England and feels that he is not able to return: 'England is nothing to me' (Dickens, 1987; 197). At this point Gill's orphanhood is absolute: he is without family, home or nation and his colonial experience has turned him into a permanent outsider. Gill does return to England and partially to his marginalised position – held there by his illiteracy: 'I was recommended for promotion, and everything was done to reward me that could be done; but my total want of all learning stood in my way, ... I could not conquer any learning, though I tried' (Dickens, 1987: 207). However, the narrative does work to ensure his reassimilation; as such, Dickens's use of the colonial frontier translates into a partial solution for problems at home. Gill is content in his service which he now respects and holds 'dear' (Dickens, 1987: 207), and which he finds respects him. Likewise, Gill's experience as colonial agent has enabled him to find a quasi-family – first with the Marines and then with the Cartons – and to affirm the domestic narrative. It is with key representatives of the navy (the sergeant who is valiant for duty's sake and the captain who is a self-sacrificing leader) that the qualities that Gill could not find in England are found in its representatives. Like his friend Harry who learns to respect the sergeant who so abused him when he sees him resolute in the face of death, Gill so admires Captain Carton that he is quite content when the woman he desires chooses to marry the captain. Gill lives with them. Finally it is with Mrs Carton that Gill finds a scribe to overcome his own illiteracy, 'write' his story and enter into the discursive arena.

The theme of the orphan as sailor continues on in the popular literature of the 1870s and 1880s; the orphan still represented as demonised other. The presence of such an other within continues to fuel the arguments of those who saw a pressing need for a Christian civilising mission within the heart of Victorian England.

One of the late orphan adventure tales, the 'Trials in the Life of an Orphan Sailor Boy' found in Volume II of *Five Sea Novels* (1871), is interesting for its demonisation of the orphan figure. Unlike the valiant and basically good figure of Gill, the orphan Lute, a shiphand, is a demonised figure who is continually abused by his drunken captain, a symbol of degenerate authority. Lute's unknown genealogy is linked to the sea. The sea was 'at once father and mother and sister and brother to him' (Anon., 1871: 110). Being linked to the sea, as opposed to land, emphasises Lute's orphanhood as the rootedness associated with land/place are central concepts to the narratives of family and nation. The captain describes Lute as threatening; one who possesses a temper akin to a 'dark passion' and possesses a nature likened to that of 'young Satan' (Anon., 1871: 109). The corporal punishment Lute suffers actually helps to reinforce this devilish nature as his resentment of the captain hardens into hatred. In fact Lute sees himself both in the position of 'prisoner' and of 'slave' to the 'tyrant' captain (Anon., 1871: 113). However, Lute's moral degeneration is halted by meeting the Captain's young child whose idealised innocence awakens in Lute a 'holy love' (Anon., 1871: 115). After rescuing this child repeatedly over the course of the narrative, they marry and thus Lute, as one neutralised and assimilated, is reintegrated back into the society.

In his ending of *Perils* Dickens therefore anticipates developments in later orphan adventure narratives. Gill's sense of alienation from England and the difficulty he has in returning can be read as a forerunner to such tales as Lizzie Glover's *Victor, The Little Orphan; Or, the Necessity of Self-Help* (1876) in which the heroism of the orphan soldier becomes the heroism of the orphan as pioneer: emigration becomes an act of self-help and a further stage in colonial endeavours. In this narrative, Victor emigrates with his sister and the two survive a number of misfortunes to become pillars of the community.

Likewise, in Gill's return and partial reinscription into english society, it is possible to identify Bowen's *Cared For; Or the Orphan Wanderers* (1881). This narrative is a reverse adventure narrative focusing on the wanderings of two orphans, Philip and Susie Arnold, who are orphaned when their mother dies during the return journey from Australia to England. This journey, now from the colonies to Victorian England, is characterised by the difficulties en route back and the threatening nature of Victorian England to her subjects. After the death of their mother the only place for the orphans in Victorian society is the workhouse. Rather than go to a workhouse, the two children set out to find their English relatives. During their travels their prolonged stay in a gypsy camp signifies their otherness. Ultimately, the children are integrated back into mainstream

Christian society but not without difficulty. This is a narrative of reverse emigration for the orphans from the Australian periphery to a British centre. But this centre is threatening to British subjects who seek their extended British family and their place within Victorian society.

4

The emigration of orphan children

In conclusion, it appears to me that in sending out these children
to Bermuda, the directors did what was for the children's good; that
their motive was a regard for their welfare; that the affair was trans-
acted with deliberation, and that the children so long as they
depended on the directors were amply provided for; but that *the
whole proceeding was illegal.* (PP, 1851, XL, 417, my italics)

THESE CONCLUSIONS, drawn in 1851 by Richard
Hall, the Poor Law Inspector conducting the inquiry into
the emigration of children to Bermuda by the Board of
Guardians of Marylebone in St Pancras parish, marked the end of one
of the first plans for systematic emigration of pauper orphans and
children to the colonies. The emigration to the colonies of orphan
children of the poor marked both a new phase in the state (parish)
provision for such children and a concerted effort to ensure the familial nature of empire by settling the colonies with British children.
The two endeavours coincide in the notion that the colonies were the
birthright of British children – hence providing a special opportunity
to a very special responsibility of the Government, the provision for
orphan children of the poor. The orphan popular adventure narratives that were furthering the work of empire were accompanied by
emigration schemes which specifically targeted the orphan figure as
an agent to help in the imperial work of settlement. Such schemes
operated in addition to the opportunities offered by the merchant
navy and the marines; such schemes conceived of empire as a familial configuration and a birthright for those for whom England could

not provide a suitable birthright – the impoverished orphans. This chapter will examine the formative moment of the emigration movement which developed over the next seventy years into a fully-fledged scheme for the emigration of orphan children. To do so it is important to examine the historical context of these particular endeavours as articulated at the time and, in retrospect, in the early twentieth-century evaluations of the scheme. Finally, the chapter will examine certain popular texts, with a special emphasis placed on Rose Macaulay's *Orphan Island* in order to show how these texts narrativise the schemes and highlight the class, ethnic, racial and sectarian debates which intersect with these schemes.

The Marylebone scheme in 1850 was the first organised scheme to emigrate orphan children under the care of a Board of Guardians. The inquiry was initiated after a newspaper report on 18 January 1851 which alleged that the Board of Guardians of Marylebone were using poor law money to emigrate children to Bermuda. The inquiry subsequently found that the plan was first initiated by a request from a Captain Thomas W.B. Burrow that he be allowed to emigrate a number of pauper children on his merchant ship into service in Bermuda. Although this particular scheme was found by the inquiry to be illegal and hence was discontinued, in reality it marked the beginning of three distinct schemes to emigrate children who were the responsibility of the Poor Law Board. This first scheme was to Bermuda, the second scheme was to New South Wales and the third, and by far the most substantial and systematic was to Canada – in particular to the provinces of Ontario and Quebec. It is important, therefore, to consider briefly each scheme separately before drawing any conclusions.

The Bermuda scheme

Captain Burrow's request to the Marylebone Board of Guardians met with significant objections. The guardians felt that as Bermuda was a penal colony, 'To dispose of children in this way is worse than to transport them' (PP, 1851, XL, 413). Despite the fact that these particular objections were laid to rest by a submission by Mr Leonard

Stewart strong reservations remained. In fact, there was unanimous agreement 'not to entertain so absurd and inhuman a proposition' and 'that they were legally and morally bound to watch over the interests of the pauper children, and not to allow them to be jeopardised by so novel a speculation' (PP, 1851, XL, 413). It is very curious then that despite these unanimous resolutions the Board ultimately agreed three groups of children to be emigrated.

The first group of children was sent in February 1850. The group was comprised of four boys aged between thirteen and sixteen years, two of whom were orphans and the other two were living in the workhouse separated from their family. They were: James George, an orphan aged thirteen; John Howlett, aged fourteen, who had a father living in the workhouse; George Chamon, an orphan aged fourteen; and James Hart, aged sixteen, who had family living in Boston. The children went on a voluntary basis; they were deemed to be in robust health and had, if appropriate, the permission of their relatives or 'friends'. For the journey the children were provided with an outfit of clothes, a bible and prayer book, a brush; a comb and 2s 6d. The master and schoolmaster accompanied the boys and verified the accommodation was very good. Captain Burrow, for his part, agreed the following conditions:

1 the children to be emigrated were to be between twelve and fourteen years of age (a condition which appears to have been breached on the very first emigration as James Hart was already sixteen);
2 for the £6 that Captain Burrow charged for passage money he was to provide bed, bedding and board for the journey for the children;
3 the children were to be conveyed as cabin passengers;
4 the girls and boys were to be keep separate throughout the journey;
5 the children were to be apprenticed as domestic servants until they were eighteen years of age;
6 Captain Burrow was required to demonstrate that he had places for them all before they embarked and to provide records of where each child was apprenticed.

There were no funds to help the children get other situations or to return to England once the apprenticeship was finished. Thus, however efficient and benevolent the motivation for emigrating these children, this was to be a one-way trip with the children indentured as apprentices until adulthood and thus removed from the charge of the parish. It was a guarantee that they would have no call on the parish as children again.

On 5 June 1850 the second party, consisting of ten boys, three girls and eight men, chosen from volunteers went out to Bermuda. Of this group all the children, except one boy, were orphans and two of the girls had brothers among the boys being sent. Again the children were outfitted by the Board, but this time the outfit was significantly more substantial.[12] The third party, sent on 10 October 1850, consisted of ten girls, nine boys and two young women between sixteen and seventeen years of age. The same provision was made for them and the same amount charged.

As far as the Board of Guardians was concerned, this project was a great success. During the inquiry the Board produced letters written by the children emigrated which testified to: the high moral character of the children sent; the regard with which the workhouse was held by these children; and the excellent opportunity which Bermuda provided for the children. As a testimonial to the children's high moral character and their advanced learning, James George wrote on 6 March 1850 requesting a ' copy of Mr Cornwell's geography' in order to 'know a little more about ciphering'. As a testimonial to the regard with which the workhouse was held and the excellent opportunities in Bermuda, James George, in the same letter sent his regards to 'former masters and friends (especially Half-a-loaf Dabtoe)' and requested that they try to send his aunt to Bermuda. In the same vein, Percival had his employer write to a friend in the workhouse urging him to come to Bermuda as he had found a place of employment for him in the Royal Naval Hospital. Percival claimed to be able to save £6 every three months. Likewise, George Baron wrote pleading that his sister be sent out and talked of the kindness of both his master and mistress 'and the good family that Samuel Thelwell is with' (PP, 1851, XL, 421–33).

Overall, the Board felt that, with this scheme, they were providing the children in their care with a tangible opportunity for the future not available in England. Despite the level of training provided by the workhouse, where English society was concerned these orphan children were tainted by their origins, and such a taint effectively prevented them from holding positions either with the most respectable families or in the community at large. Despite the success recorded by the workhouse masters in placing the children in their care, their reports and those of the HMI school inspectors recorded the number of times workhouse children lost positions if their background was revealed. 'The stigma of having been brought up under the Poor Law – which, notwithstanding the assertions of the Poor Law Commission to the contrary, is a very real one ... Only the other day the public read of a woman who was driven from house to house by her neighbours discovering that she was once a "workhouse girl"' (Crane, 1915: 124).

Thus, this emigration scheme was seized on as being 'the means of rendering happy many who would otherwise have no chance in England of leaving the workhouse, and would continue to be a burthen on the parish' (PP, 1851, XL, 425). It was also, in the words of Osmond Jones, whose family had been in the Bermudas for several generations, a chance of 'bettering their condition, instead of being apprenticed in England, and sometimes, as I have heard, returning with their masters to the workhouse when their apprenticeship expires' (PP, 1851, XL, 425). Jones was undoubtedly referring to the fact that apprenticeships for the children were often found among the poor working community who would be paid to take a child; such a community struggled for existence and often only the money paid for the apprenticeship helped to keep members out of the workhouse. Once the apprentice's money was finished, the master could not afford to keep him on, or pay him wages, but might himself have to go to the workhouse because he was so impoverished. True, the Board of Guardians conceived this scheme of emigration as literally providing the best care and opportunity for those, particularly the orphans, who were in their care, but one cannot ignore the reality that by making a one-off payment for the passage of these pauper orphans the Board of Guardians could reduce the numbers for which they had to provide out of the poor rates and thus economise at a time when the claims on the poor rates were increasing. It was a supplementary economy at work here, in its infrastructural sense of the term, in which orphans in particular were identified as surplus, a financial burden to be got rid of. It was an economy which benefited both the Boards of Guardians in England and the colonies. Not only did Captain Burrow make a profit out of his human cargo, but also Bermuda received new bodies for service and to bolster a decreasing population.

In the midst of celebrating the success of the emigration scheme a letter arrived from B.S. Matthew, dated 6 August 1850, which stated that, now that he was a man, he was unable to find employment in Bermuda and thus he was now obliged, as was his friend Nimmor, to emigrate further to Toronto, Canada. Thus, despite the assurances of both Captain Burrow that he had positions secured for all whom he was paid to emigrate and Mr Birmingham, a director of the Board of Guardians, that Bermuda's decreasing population created a demand for workers to emigrate, it appears that neither were strictly accurate. B.S. Matthew having been emigrated was now without any right to return passage. Unable to find work, providing for his own subsistence must have been difficult (there were no poor laws in Bermuda at the time); it is a wonder that he was able to provide for his passage to Canada.[13] The letter was also an ominous forecast of the possible fate in store for the orphan children once their indentures were finished. What would become of those who were not able to save money, unlike Percival quoted above, once their indentures ceased?

Although Matthew and Nimmor's situation appears to have been an isolated incident, there were other more fundamental areas of concern which only became public during the inquiry in 1851: the foremost was the issue of consent. As the children themselves were almost always orphans or deserted children under the age of sixteen their legal consent was required. However, the inquiry revealed that such consent was not always obtained in the required manner. Under the law of the time the consent of the children was to be obtained in petty sessions; thus, a certificate verified by two justices would be needed prior to embarkation (13 & 14 Vict., c.101, s.4). During the verification the two judges would have separately interviewed the child in question to ensure that she or he understood what they were doing and the ramifications of their decision. This was not obtained for any of the children; the Board only obtained their own verbal consent. Also, the inquiry found that the directors funded this emigration from the poor rate without having obtained the 'order and confirmation of the Poor-law Board, as required by [law] the 4 & 5 Will.4, c.76, s.62, and the 7 & 8 Vict., c.101, s.29. The expenditure out of the poor rate was therefore 'illegal in regard to the whole of the emigration' (PP, 1851, XL, 430).

The New South Wales scheme

In many ways the early emigration scheme to Bermuda formed a prototype for the very substantial emigration scheme to Canada which started in the 1870s. Despite the fact that the largest number of orphan emigrants went to Canada, in a scheme modelled on the Bermuda plan, Canada and Bermuda are almost entirely excluded in critical work today. Instead, the most common area of inquiry focuses on the emigration schemes to Australia (Hughes, 1987; Hassam, 1994). One can only speculate why this is so. Certainly several high profile schemes of emigration involving major public figures are sources of interest; Dickens and Angela Burdett-Coutts's Home for Fallen Women and its links with emigration to Australia has garnered significant attention (Collins, 1965). However, even this bears some further examination. If one looks carefully at the communication between the President of the Poor Law Board and the Emigration Commissioners in 1854–55, it becomes apparent that certain categories of people were ineligible to emigrate, namely: families who had been in receipt of parish relief; women over thirty-five years of age; and women with illegitimate children. In addition, those emigrating must not only have been in good health and 'free from bodily or mental defects' but must have been able to provide certificates verifying that they were 'sober, industrious, of general good moral character and have been in the habit of working for wages' (PP, 1854–55, XLVI, 65). These conditions must have presented a problem for schemes such as Urania Cottage's emigration of reformed fallen women and for the poor labouring classes who must inevitably have needed to claim parish relief, if even only outdoor, at one time or other. The question remains how Dickens, Angela Burdett-Coutts and others managed to work around this requirement; they would have been able to testify to the reformed nature of the women they were sending, having supervised their rehabilitation, yet how could they certify that these women were in the habit of working for wages and had never had an illegitimate child or received parish relief? The New South Wales scheme differed from the other schemes in that while it welcomed working women of good character under thirty-five years of age it did not accept female orphans under eighteen unless they were going into the care of immediate relatives. Thus, as far as the New South Wales scheme was concerned the work of settling empire was perceived as a man's – or in this case, a boy's job.

But this is to take attention away from the main focus of this study. A significant number of women that Dickens and Burdett-Coutts helped were raised in workhouses and were probably orphans (Walkowitz, 1980: 3). But this emigration scheme also involved emigrating pauper children, both orphans and non-orphans, to New South Wales (NSW). The total cost of the fare to NSW was £20 with £8 being paid by the NSW government to encourage the emigration of a cheap workforce and £12 paid by the Board of Guardians responsible for the child. The conditions for being chosen for emigration were similar to those of the aborted Bermuda scheme: the boys must be over thirteen years of age; they must have the permission of the parents or Board of Guardians; and an employer must be secured before the children set sail. As with the Bermuda scheme the actual legal requirement that a certificate must be produced, signed by two magistrates verifying that the children understood the ramifications of their decision, was seldom carried out. Similarly, the ticket was for a one-way trip to indentured labour with no provision being made for return. Again, the Guardians thought that they were providing their charges with an opportunity of better future prospects than were available in England while at the same time reducing the numbers claiming on their poor rates. Underlying the infrastructural sense of the supplementary economy in which the orphan is identified as a financial burden, it is possible to identify a superstructure – an ideology which identifies the orphan as a *pharmakon*: an excess to be excluded, an outsider who is relegated to the outside: the confines of the empire. Derrida captures this ideology in his delineation of the pharmakon as that to be: 'excluded – expelled or cut off from the social arena. ... It is thus necessary to put the outside back in its place. To keep the outside out' (Derrida, 1981: 97–128).

The Canada scheme

While the Bermuda scheme was predominantly focused on the emigration of orphan children from the workhouse, the NSW scheme sought to emigrate not only orphan boys, but also poor families and surplus women. In 1870, two philanthropic women, Miss Rye and Miss Macpherson started a scheme to emigrate 'street arabs' (the children of costermongers and street traders who wandered the streets bereft of education and suitable clothing and who were orientalised in a discourse which labelled them arabs) and pauper orphan children to Canada. The category of 'street arabs' also included 'waifs and strays', and 'gutter children' – both male and female.

In an attempt to differentiate this scheme from other endeavours both previous and current, the emigration agents professed to act as parents to the orphan and neglected children of the poor. The professed aim of Miss Rye and Miss Macpherson was to act as 'parents to these rescued children, rather than simple emigration agents to supply the labour market ... by taking a lifelong interest in those we sought to assist, recording their well-doing or their ill-doing upon our books, assisting the weak and the sick, rewarding the industrious, and giving wholesome advice and training to those who fall back to their old habits' (PP, 1875, LXIII, 259). Although the Guardians of a few unions sent out children with Miss Rye in 1869 (the first Union to do so was Kirkdale Union in Liverpool who sent fifty children), it was not until 1870 that the Poor Law Board sanctioned, by order, the emigration of pauper children to Canada under the care of Miss Rye and Miss Macpherson, a sanction which greatly facilitated the emigration of pauper children. Previous to this a contract with shippers, much like the one used in the Bermuda scheme, was used to emigrate pauper children from unions. The mixing of the category of pauper children who had been brought up in the workhouse (and thus segregated from these other children) and the 'arabs' eventually causes concern for the Government Board responsible for the pauper children.

In the first four years of the scheme approximately 1150 pauper children were sent out, paid for by the rates. The number of 'arabs' was much larger. Miss Rye claims that their scheme rescues 'the fatherless, motherless, friendless, and bedless ... [whose sole possession was often] only one garment retaining the form of a shirt and two pairs of boots' (PP, 1875, LXIII, 259) from their 'homes' of 'the night asylum, the police office, cold stairs, haylofts, and barrels and boxes along the harbour.' The aim was to remove the children from the 'evil influences' to which they had been exposed (PP, 1875, LXIII, 261). Although Miss Macpherson identifies her work as simultaneously parental and 'of a missionary character',[14] Andrew Doyle in his report to the Local Government Board investigating the conditions in Canada in which the children were living makes clear that this endeavour was to be understood as 'an agency for the promotion of emigration' (PP, 1875, LXIII, 259). Both the ladies and the agencies took out the same class of children and distributed them on the same principles, and both obtained funds for subscriptions from Guardians, the Government of the Dominion, and province of Ontario, to cover their costs. There were homes established to receive these orphan and deserted children in Peckham, Hampton, Liverpool, Edinburgh, Glasgow and Dublin; the children were sent to receiving homes at Knowlton, Quebec, Belleville, Niagara and Galt Ontario for resettlement in Ontario and Quebec. By the time of Doyle's report in 1875 a large number of children, both 'arab' and 'pauper' had been sent out by these two ladies as emigrants to Canada and several other persons had started similar endeavours.

The children sent out were of all ages, from infancy (for adoption into Canadian families) to fifteen years of age. Eventually, 'arab' and pauper children were joined by children from the reformatories.

Although Rye and Macpherson were the first to offer a systematic emigration scheme to Canada for orphan and street children they were by no means the only ones. In 1873 Dr T. Bowman Stephenson (the founder of the National Children's Home and Orphanage) established a receiving home at Hamilton, Ontario and the following year emigrated his first party of boys. Stephenson quickly established a reputation for doing a work 'altogether superior in character' and producing 'sturdy and successful citizens' (Crane, 1915: 20).

Opposition to these schemes came from various sources. There was an unease about the emigration scheme as 'confession of [the] failure' of both the Boards of Guardians to care for the most vulnerable of those entrusted to them and the state to eradicate poverty and suffering of its subjects. The Guardians stated that they were 'loath to transfer to the shoulders of strangers the burden of their responsibility' and that 'the abolition of pauperism must find its fulfilment in our own land,' on which account 'the brunt of our battle has to be fought *here.*' (Crane, 1915: 136).

Employers and capitalists whose profits and viability depended on the readily available source of cheap labour also voiced objections to the emigration scheme; the orphan children provided a significant supply of cheap labour. In addition, the emphasis on the need to emigrate only the most healthy and able-bodied to the colonies was seen to deplete the labour pool and hence was viewed with concern: the emigration of fit and able orphan children was seen as depleting the 'best children ... [with whom the employers and capitalists] can least afford to part' (Crane, 1915: 138).

Contrary to the early emigration scheme to Bermuda, conditions on the journey to Canada were often unsatisfactory. There was inadequate supervision for the needs of the children (in some journeys there were 150 children sent with one guardian). As a result, personal cleanliness was much neglected during the voyage and often there was no care for the children when they were ill. Children told Doyle of vomiting over each other and being left to lie in it; adults receiving the children told of their 'heads swarming with vermin' (PP, 1875, LXIII, 272). On their arrival, Doyle found that there was no suitable provision for the reception and employment of children arriving. The Western Home in Niagara was cited as a specific example, it was a home which slept 120 children but the offices, washing accommodation, etc. 'falls short of that required in an English workhouse' (PP, 1875, LXIII, 261–3). Almost all of the homes visited had 'inadequate provision' to ensure that male and female children were separated.

However, the proponents of the emigration schemes argued that reducing the cost of parish relief by reducing the numbers on the lists should not be the primary consideration, rather that the state should have the welfare of their charges at heart. The provision of a fresh start in the colonies where the taint of the workhouse origins would not prevail was argued to be in the children's best interest:

> The State is hardly ideal in her relationships with her children when her chief consideration is what they cost and how that cost can be reduced to the barest minimum. ...
>
> The immediate duty of the State to the innocent victims of circumstance is, obviously, as far as possible to cut off the entail of their misfortune. They must be saved from the taint of pauperism.
> (Crane, 1915: 123)

However, if seen as stigmatised the orphans become scapegoats who carry their unknown origins and poverty like guilt. The expelling of such figures to the colonies was an act of double effacement: it erased both the orphans' unknown origins and the cause of their poverty.

Thus, emigration, predictably, is seen as an act of self-help; Canadians in general were viewed as evidence of the potential success of this ideal: 'Too many Canadian families are themselves of lowly origin, too many of the social leader have themselves risen from obscurity, to attach undue importance to birth and breeding. The self-made man is the national ideal, and the humbler the origin the more creditable the rise' (Crane, 1915: 124).

Doyle's report was not only critical of the operation but ultimately he adopted the view that the Guardians should discontinue this scheme. There were several issues which caused concern. First and foremost, contrary to Rye and Macpherson's claim to act as parents, in a unique humanitarian endeavour, they did not. Self-promotion aside, one of the stipulations by the Board of Guardians was that Rye and Macpherson were to act as the legal guardians of the orphan children. Not only did Rye and Macpherson fail to do so regarding the children in Canada, but there was no attempt on the part of the Canadian officials to verify that children brought in had been put under legal care of the two; thus, Rye and Macpherson – or any other emigration agents for that matter – could have been bringing in children illegally. Doyle identified a legal loophole that could possibly have resulted in the illegal emigration of children: 'Indeed there appears to be nothing in the laws of either England or of Canada to prevent any person of a philanthropic or speculative turn, who can collect money for the purpose, from gathering any number of "waifs and strays and street arabs" and with their easily obtained consent shipping them to Canada, and through Canada to the States' (PP, 1875, LXIII, 264). The entire scheme was unregulated and unmonitored and thus, abuses or actions by unscrupulous persons emigrating children without their or their parents' consent were a possibility.

In addition, once in Canada, Rye and Macpherson did not fulfil their role as guardians. In fact, the entire system of placement was inadequate. First, when reviewing the scheme Doyle found that very few records exist on the distribution of children (unlike the work-house system where the masters claimed to be able to provide information on the whereabouts of the majority of their inmates and often inquired into their condition). This inadequacy was compounded by the nature of the work undertaken. First, because there was plenty of opportunity for agricultural labourers, the children frequently change situation (at times without Miss Rye's approval or even knowledge) and hence monitoring became impossible. Second, contrary to the painstaking process undertaken by the workhouse masters in England, in Canada, Rye and Macpherson placed the children rapidly and without proper assessment; as this was often their first employment it literally doomed the children to failure. The inspector concluded that: 'If Miss Rye and Miss

Macpherson were less anxious to get the children off their hands immediately upon arrival, not only would they be able to exercise greater discrimination in selecting places, but they would be able to get them out upon better terms' (PP, 1875, LXIII, 274). Once placed the children were not properly supervised. Since the children were neither trained nor acclimatised properly before being sent to work they were often repeatedly unsuccessful in their placements. Third, most worryingly, Rye and Macpherson at times relied on others to distribute the children, often with undesirable results. Finally, Doyle concluded that 'the homes should be seen, but they are not seen. The truth appears to be that in this respect, as in others, the work has rapidly outgrown the means provided for carrying it on, assuming that the means were sufficient at the outset' (PP, 1875, LXIII, 274). Without such care, as has been accepted by the Poor Law Board in 1870 with regard to boarding-out in England, 'great abuses are quite certain to ensue'. Indeed, in Canada 'it is very certain that great abuses do ensue' (PP, 1875, LXIII, 273). Such abuses included boys being brought back because the master 'drank', because 'he was with rough men and learning to swear', for being 'too small', and because 'the people were not kind to them' (PP, 1875, LXIII, 274).

This was such a change from a workhouse system that prided itself on its continued paternal care of inmates both past and present and that invested a special responsibility and a special potential in its orphan children – the very children it shipped off to the colonies for an opportunity of a new life. In fact, Doyle found himself 'unable to recognise any very marked contrast between the condition of pauper children in Canada and of the same class in England' (PP, 1875, LXIII, 275). Ultimately, the report concluded that union children were received with 'the brand upon them with which they are often so unjustly marked in England ... presented to the people of Canada as objects of pity, to be taken into service as much for charity as for what their labour is worth' (PP, 1875, LXIII, 275).

Rye and Macpherson were emigrating children of all ages, including very young ones. In 1871 Miss Rye sought to justify the need to emigrate children as young as five or six years old to Canada.

There are three distinct sets of people who apply to me for the children. ... There are those who apply from the very highest motives, *viz.*, pity for orphan children, and a desire to be fellow workers with fellow Christians here who are desiring to lessen the amount of sin and suffering among children in England. This class is limited, but a large class still in Canada, as Christian works are necessarily limited in a country where there is very little sickness, no poverty, or destitution. ... There are those who, having married young, and whose children have followed their example, find themselves at comparatively an early age, say 45, childless and alone in life with more than they want in every sense of the word, to whom a young child in the house is a boon and a blessing. ... There are those who require children on account of their services, and who willingly take them on account of their future usefulness. (PP, 1875, LXIII, 266)

But in reality those wanting to adopt a child made up no more than ten per cent of those who requested children, the majority who took the children on to put them to work at a young age. (PP, 1875, LXIII, 266–7). The children placed in domestic service fared the worst, often placed in situations 'worse than a Board of Guardians would consent to place a child in England' (PP, 1875, LXIII, 268). Findings of this sort were very serious for the Board of Guardians in England as they entrusted children, for whose care they were legally responsible, to a person who was providing less than they would have received in England. Most significantly, adoption became synonymous with exploitation. Only a small percentage of children emigrated were actually adopted in the traditional sense of the word; a large number were supposedly 'adopted' but in reality this means that they worked without wages and were subject to the authority of their 'foster' parents. In this sense, the foster parents were only required to provide maintenance and clothing until they were eighteen. In the words of one unknown girl: 'Doption sir, is when folks gets a girl to work without wages' (PP, 1875, LXIII, 266). In conjunction with this the indentures under which the majority of children were placed were in reality 'worthless or delusive. To the employer it afforded no security for the service of the child: to the child it afforded no protection' (PP, 1875, LXIII, 266).

Also, in England the inmates of workhouses were classified so as to prevent children from being 'contaminated' by the 'immorality' and 'degeneration' of the adult paupers and to prevent the orphan and deserted children from being corrupted in school by the vices learnt by the children of pauper parents at a young age. Yet, in Canada, the pauper orphans were being indiscriminately mixed with a large proportion of children who were 'semi-criminals of our large cities and towns' (PP, 1875, LXIII, 268) who had little or no education or industrial training. So it appears that all the efforts to rescue this special group of children from precisely this fate were being undone in the land of opportunity to which they were being sent. Despite the fact that the Local Government Board originally assented to the scheme on the understanding that the children would be emigrated and spend a further amount of time in a receiving home for more industrial training, this was never done. Instead, for too many 'the change was simply of country and climate, not of habits and character' (PP, 1875, LXIII, 270). As a result, children were ill prepared for the situations in which they were suddenly placed and there was no attention paid to matching children with suitable employers. One result was that the scheme quickly became discredited 'through the incapacity, unfitness, ... [and] gross misconduct of many of the children who are sent out' (PP, 1875, LXIII, 270). The Warden of the county of Hastings, Ontario stated, 'It would take a long time ... to eradicate the evil that had been produced in his own immediate neighbourhood by the class of children who had been imported into it' (PP, 1875, LXIII, 269).

Crucially, emigration effectively removed all state support for which the children were eligible if they remained in England.

> People who promote the emigration of children should bear in mind that in Canada there are no poor laws. Even those who contend that a country, especially a new country, will get on better without them cannot but admit that orphan and deserted children sent out as emigrants stand in altogether an exceptional position, and should not be deprived of that help in distress that the law would have given them had they not been removed from their own country. It appears to be but reasonable that up to a certain age

every child should be entitled to admission to, and support, when 'destitute' in the Home from which it may have been sent into service, of course under strict conditions as should guard the right from being abused, or from operating as an inducement to idleness or misconduct. (PP, 1875, LXIII, 272)

This lack of support comes to light in many forms: e.g., Doyle discovered a boy being ill-used in service in Canada and found destitute sitting on a box. Other cases of maltreatment included: objectionable sleeping quarters; children not properly clothed for the Canadian winter; children not receiving the education agreed as a condition of their being placed; children being sent to a Sunday school not of their denomination; cases of ill-treatment and hardship which involve the withholding of food, and flogging marks still visible on one child a fortnight after being administered (PP, 1875, LXIII, 283). Young female orphans suffered particular abuse – often resulting in unwanted pregnancy. Doyle came across women who subsequently gave birth to illegitimate children and lacked any social support whatsoever. He discovered a girl of thirteen who had been horsewhipped. He also discovered a girl who lost the sight of one eye because of the careless use of firearms by the children of the family. The sense of exile experienced by these children is expressed poignantly in the letter of one of the female emigrants (known only as S.M.):

> Dear Sir, – I write to tell you that I would very much like to see you on Wednesday, but no, I cannot anymore have the heart to go to Marchmont [one of the Receiving Homes], for it has never been a home for me, although it was told to me and all the rest, that when we came to Canada it was to be a home. But, Sir, I have known the time when I would have been glad for a bit to eat and a bed to lie on, for I my own self have had to sleep in barns for a shelter when the snow have been so thick, and no person would be seen out, and have been to Marchmont for a shelter, and was turned away, so that I have nothing to thank them for. If I had only taken my parents' advice I would have not been here, but as long as they can bring out poor children to be pounded half to death, and slave to the uttermost, that is all they care for. I know —— has got me several places, and me not know how to do their work as they did; they

would scold, and offer to strike me, and of course I would leave; and another thing, I was not going to be told that I was glad to come to Canada, for I was half starved, and was picked off the streets in London, and my parents were drunkards. Dear Sir, nobody knows what a girl has to put up with that comes from the old country, for they know we have no parents to take our part, and they can do as they like. ... I always tried to do what I could, and every time I went to ——, she would always be scolding and telling me things what folks said about me, and I always thought I would not try to do right anymore, for nobody cared for me; for there was a time when I was sick, and had all my clothes taken away to pay for my board, and only one dress to cover me, and was obliged to borrow money to get clothing with. I have been in Canada three years, and have worked my way through sorrow and woe, and can do so still, even when we were so far away from our parents. They would not let me see the only sister I had, and there is many more just like me, so when I get better and able to go to work, I am going to New London, and I was a very foolish girl to leave England, for I had a good home if it was an orphan's home. (PP, 1875, LXIII, 279)

In addition, the respectable employers complained that no one took any interest in the children placed; often as many as four years elapsed between visits. Although Miss Macpherson states that they did not 'set the little emigrant afloat, ... [letting] him "paddle his own canoe" on the ocean of life, inquiring no farther as to his "welfare"', Doyle concluded that 'this, unhappily, is just what has been done. The little emigrants have been set afloat, and too many of them let to "paddle their own canoes" until, as Miss Macpherson might express it, some of them have gone over the rapids, and others are already lost sight of in the great human tide of the Western cities' (PP, 1875, LXIII, 276). If they were not lost sight of in the cities, the children were just as likely to end up in the penitentiary.

Overall, the loss of state support and the possibility of abuse made the child's informed consent even more imperative. However, as with the Bermuda scheme, this consent was not properly obtained before the child was shipped out. The inspector observed: 'I met with several cases of children sent out as "orphans" who had one if not both parents living' (PP, 1875, LXIII, 261). (Rye and Macpherson worked under the definition that any child deserted for more than three years was an orphan, cf., 'Memorandum' in Appendix.) Under the pretence of providing opportunity the scheme attempted to rid the country of children labelled 'evil' or 'expendable' (this tag being applicable to those under the State's care who cost the parish money) while providing a cheap labour force for the development of the colony. In this supplementary economy, orphanhood became a malleable category; it became a means of identifying marginalised, dispossessed and so-called undesirables. This figure of the orphan was invested with the poison of the *pharmakon*. The pharmaceutical nature of the supplementary economy ensured that such poison was expelled to the colonies; such expulsion was simultaneously a cure for the need to settle the colonies with white settlers. However, this expulsion was in fact a process of exile. The experience of exile truly began once the orphan turned eighteen and hence was no longer the official responsibility of the representatives of the Board. Then the emigrants 'find themselves without friends or advisers and, as a rule, without associations that attach them to families or to neighbour-hoods in which they are known' (PP, 1875, LXIII, 275). Referring to the quote from *Daniel Deronda* with which I opened this book, these are the very elements seen to comprise a sense of familial, community and national belonging. Thus, their orphanhood becomes absolute; their sense of national belonging has been taken, and they are foreigners in the new country. This misery of exile and enforced foreignness works against Derrida's linkage of writing with vagrancy (and orphanhood) in order to celebrate such a state as democratic:[15]

> Writing is ... also like someone who has lost his right, an outlaw, a pervert, a bad seed, a vagrant, an adventurer, a bum. *Wandering in the streets, he doesn't even know who he is, what is identity – if he has one – might be, what his name is, what his father's name is.* ... *He can no longer repeat his origin.* Not to know where one comes from or where one is going, for a discourse with no guarantor, is not to know how to speak at all, to be in a state of infancy. *Uprooted, anonymous, unattached to any house or country, this almost insignificant signifier is at everyone's disposal ... At the disposal of each and of all, available on the sidewalks, isn't writing thus essentially democratic?*. (Derrida, 1981: 143–4, my italics)

In this passage, one can identify the state of orphanhood as that in which one can no longer repeat one's origin. In Victorian culture, orphanhood did become a signifier at everyone's disposal in a discourse which identified it as the excess to be excluded. How then in exile and a foreigner, 'uprooted, unattached to any house or country' is the orphan to enjoy the democratic rights Derrida celebrates? I want to make it perfectly clear here that I borrow the model of the *pharmakon* because of the usefulness of the ambivalence it embodies for a conceptualisation of the orphan. However, I do not share Derrida's celebration of vagrancy; one must not overlook the destitution and deprivation of the orphan at the time. The orphan's homelessness and suffering was a real social, economical concern rather than metaphysical playfulness.

In conclusion, the report suggested that, given the contempt and pity these children faced in Canada, 'it would surely be better to keep them at home, letting them take their chance of what Guardians can do for them amongst their own people' (PP, 1875, LXIII, 275). The schemes were condemned by many public figures in England, notably Lord Shaftesbury who wrote in *The Times* a few years later in 1877: 'With children of this class it is not enough merely to launch them on the sea of life. Parentless, most of them, and friendless, they must have someone to advise them how to improve their advantages, but still more someone to counsel and assist them in circumstances of difficulty or temptation' (PP, 1877, LXXI, 5). However, it is important to note that the concern for pauper children expressed by Shaftesbury and others really referred to the pauper orphan and deserted children who lived in the workhouse – a special class. No such parental responsibility can be detected for the children of the reformatories and industrial schools, many of whom were also orphans. Instead these orphans were subjected to horrific conditions: *The Times* published on 19 August 1876 a report which revealed that in 898 children absconded from, and 719 children died in, reformatories in England, while 68 children absconded from, and 147 died in, certified industrial schools (cf., Carpenter, 1968: 1–57).

Yet the outcome of these children, often being far from what was promised, did not prevent Miss Macpherson making an earnest appeal to these very children to provide £5 so that by the next spring 'we may have the joy of starting off a thousand young hopefuls from our dens of vice' to Canada (PP, 1875, LXIII, 1875). And so one cannot ignore the issue of profit: pauper children's passage and preliminary board was paid for jointly by the Board of Guardians and the Canadian government. Why then did Miss Rye and Miss Macpherson need to raise further money? Indeed, the case was even more questionable than this; at the time public charges were levelled in the Canadian press and elsewhere that Miss Rye and Miss Macpherson had a 'pecuniary interest' in the scheme.

> It is alleged that at present the cost of conveying a pauper child from Liverpool to its destination in Ontario cannot exceed one third of the sum paid on that account by the Guardians. This no doubt would be the case if Miss Macpherson and Miss Rye avail themselves of the 'assisted passage' given by the Government of the Dominion, as well as the drawback of six dollars for each emigrant given by the Ontario Government. [... preliminary indications are that] there would be a clear gain of £5 per head upon every pauper child taken by these ladies as emigrants to Canada' and this amount would increase if the assisted passage fare were reduced (which is most likely). (PP, 1875, LXIII, 287–8)

In addition, the children were often landed, lodged and fed by the charity of the town and then taken to the market to be chosen by sight. But the Board of Guardians had paid eight guineas per head to provide for this! Furthermore, the children were sent on the assumption that they would spend a period of time in a Receiving Home for industrial training and would then be placed in a pre-arranged and pre-inspected situation. Even worse, the children were then 'invited' to repay their passage (£6 or £7 named) under the pretence of enabling another child to come – although the Board of Guardians would still have paid for this. Clearly, there was a significant profit to be made and given that by Miss Rye's own account in December 1877 that she had crossed the Atlantic 'some twenty times in six years' (PP, 1877, LXXI, 26) it is clear that large numbers of children were being emigrated.

Although the scheme of emigration of pauper orphans to Canada receives little critical attention today, it was advocated as preferential to other schemes for a number of very significant reasons regarding the future 'face of empire' – not the least of which were anxieties around race and miscegenation. Although Froude in his *Short Studies on Great Subjects*, in the chapter entitled 'England's War' argued that 'A continued stream of young, well-taught, unspoilt English natures would be the most precious gift which the colonies could receive from us' (Froude, 1872: 510), it quickly became obvious that some colonies were to be preferred over others on racial grounds. Miss Rye herself objected to the emigration of pauper children to the Cape (now South Africa) because of the 'great preponderance there of coloured people' (PP, 1877, LXXI, 22 (4)); she frankly admitted that the reasons for her choosing Canada as the recipient colony were not only ones of easy access (the journey was rarely longer than fourteen days and often only ten days) and the absence of great wealth ('neither poverty nor riches' of contentment), but primarily had to do with the settlement of the white race. She wrote of a country whose people (white people not the indigenous, black loyalist, or Asian populations) claimed a 'residence [... of] generations' and who crucially, given her objection to the settlements in the Cape, experience 'the freedom from admixture of races' (PP, 1877, LXXI, 23).

The schemes which were adopted as a method both to provide for the orphan population and to ensure the familial nature of empire by populating the colonies with white children emigrated female as well as male orphans. The female participants in this scheme deserves some attention. The emigration of young orphan women to the colonies (as part of the notion of surplus women) played a special role in this familial nature of empire as they were sent over to marry young colonists and populate the colonies with 'good white stock'. Young female orphans were first emigrated to Bermuda in 1850 as part of the short-lived scheme of the Board of Guardians of Marylebone in St Pancras parish. The emigration scheme was perceived as especially important for the young females who often, in England, faced a life of hardship and possible immorality. The Marylebone workhouse chaplain endorsed the scheme as 'a rescue and great blessing' for the young females (PP, 181, XL, 419). The emigration of female orphans was seen as an especially long-term policy as it would reduce the number of children produced in England while simultaneously providing new bodies for service to bolster a decreasing colonial population in the colonies. In conclusion, in 1875 Doyle advised that:

> If the emigration of pauper children to Canada is to continue, it should be wholly disconnected with the emigration of arab children [who] are represented without distinction as the offspring of thieves and vagabonds just swept from the slums of our great cities. Occasionally indeed the pauper children are referred to as a distinct class, but only as being 'the refuse of our workhouses'. Irrespective of the great injustice of so characterising these children, ... it tends materially to prejudice their position in service. (PP, 1875, LXIII, 289)

The concerns, which Doyle raised in his report of 1875, were addressed to a certain extent. For instance, the whole issue of inspection of children in their situations in Canada was legislated for and became much more rigorous. With regard to child emigrants generally, provincial legislation in Canada enacted after Doyle's report obliged the society emigrating the children regularly to inspect them; in the case of Poor Law children this inspection was supplemented by Canadian government inspection. These inspections were more rigorous than those Doyle examined.

> The carefulness of the Dominion agents' inspection is shown by the detailed reports – a separate one for each child – sent to Ottawa. They deal with the length of time the child has been with his employer, the nature of the work he has to do, the character of the home and its surroundings, his health, his progress and suitability for farm work, his appearance, his clothing, his attendance at day school, Sunday school and church, and, in the case of younger children, his 'behaviour' and disposition,' and – the distinction is a nice one – in that of older boys, his 'character'.
>
> Each document gives also the terms of the indenture or agreement and records any complaints made by the child or by the people with whom he is placed. Duplicate copies are forwarded from Ottawa to the Local Government Board in London, in batches

of two or three hundred, as soon as possible after receipt. (Crane,
1915: 164)

The inspections also revealed that there has been a 'marked improve-
ment' in school attendance since Doyle's day. In fact, Dr Barnardo's
paid $5 a month in order to ensure the attendance of the children that
they placed in school. Along similar lines, the repayment of passage
money ceased to be compulsory; the emigration societies now
contented themselves with soliciting 'occasional contributions', but
respected the wish of a number of orphan children to hide both their
orphanhood and the circumstances under which they came to
Canada. In addition to the inspections, the Canadian government
was more actively involved in ensuring that these emigrant children
found the adjustment to Canada as painless as possible. To this end,
social workers became part of the support network in Canada; the
aim of such work being 'preventive rather than remedial' (Crane,
1915: 168–93).

Also, children were given more thorough agricultural training
prior to emigration at homes such as the Edgeworth branch of The
National Children's Home and Orphanage. Such training ensured
that the children were equipped with the necessary skills for their
labour in Canada and thus were less likely to run away through disaf-
fection – as was the case with those emigrated in the earlier schemes
which discredited the movement in general. Finally, the Canadian
government was actively involved in supporting the emigration
scheme: in the early years of the twentieth century the Canadian
government spent 'upwards of half a million pounds on her immigra-
tion propaganda' in the United Kingdom in order to counter 'the
curious ignorance' that prevailed about life in Canada (Crane, 1915:
184). However, in 1877 Doyle, still dissatisfied, concluded that this
scheme should be discontinued for children of the poor.

Yet ultimately, despite the grave misgivings of one of the inspectors of the local government board and the serious issues raised, this
scheme was not discontinued. Rather, it was expanded and continued well into the twentieth century. An Act of 1879 further
empowered the Boards of Guardians, providing they had the consent
of the Local Government Board, 'to subscribe to any Association or

Society for aiding boys and girls in service' (e.g., the Association for Befriending Boys, the Girls' Friendly Society, and the Metropolitan Association for Befriending Young Servants) (Crane, 1915: 118). The orphan still continued to be a central figure associated with the scheme, which continued to be justified as helping a very special and vulnerable figure achieve new opportunities. As late as 1915, Dennis Crane wrote in *John Bull's Surplus Children: A Plea for Giving Them a Fairer Chance* that 'the cause of the orphan, as of all destitute or neglected children … is borne in upon us under new aspects and with new poignancy' as a 'timely' and 'urgent' subject (Crane, 1915: v). Child emigration had been in full operation since those early days of 1870 and by 1915 'upward of 65,000 orphaned or destitute British boys and girls have found new homes overseas' (Crane, 1915: 18).

Proponents of the emigration scheme argued for the urgent need to continue this work based on the numbers of orphans still under the guardianship of their home parish. On 1 January 1913 there were more than 70,000 children receiving indoor relief in England and Wales. Of these 10,000 were in district or separate schools, 11,000 were boarded out in families, 22,000 were in Cottage and other Homes, 22,000 were in workhouses, infirmaries and sick asylums. There were 29,000 children under 16 in correctional facilities. In addition to these children there were over 20,000 children in orphanages and other charitable institutions – there were 2,200 in the National Children's Home and Orphanage alone. The orphan population became so significant that they were conceived of as an 'unfortunate' class who were the 'objects of peculiar care' yet nevertheless 'start life under a considerable handicap' (Crane, 1915: 31). The orphan population was considered as distinct from those families dependent on parish relief in that the National Children's Home and Orphanage 'received a considerable proportion of its children from respectable homes that would proudly refuse any form of charity had not calamity, in the shape of death of one or both parents, come upon them' (Crane, 1915: 38). Orphanhood continued to be a vehicle for emigration; in 1912, of 2,034 children emigrated 578 had lost their mother, 509 had lost their father, and 58 had lost both of their parents.

In general, by the early twentieth century there were five principal agencies involved in the emigration of British juveniles: the Board of Guardians who were authorised by the Poor Law Amendment Act of 1870; the industrial schools who operated with the consent of the Secretary of State; the Petty Session Courts who, under the authority of the Children's Act of 1908 and with the consent of the Home Secretary, removed children from unfit parents; and benevolent enterprises and philanthropic institutions – known as emigration societies. The agents of the latter two categories were: the National Children's Home; the Church of England Waifs and Strays Society, Roman Catholic Rescue Societies; the Fegan Homes; Dr Barnardo's; National Incorporated Association; the Central Refuge and allied institutions; the Orphan Homes of Scotland; Children's Aid Society; and the Children Emigration Society (which was started by Rhodes Scholars in Oxford in 1909 to train emigrant orphans in farm schools in their land of adoption). Her younger sister, Mrs Louisa Birt, in conjunction with Sheltering Home, continued Miss Macpherson's work. Finally, there was the Junior Imperial Migration movement which was concerned exclusively with the emigration of town lads and thus was established in most of the urban centres with an especial concentration in London. Overall, if an orphan child was not emigrated then s/he was either maintained in district or 'barrack' schools, or boarded out or placed in cottages and in scatter homes (a mixture of the barrack schools and cottages where the children were maintained in homes by guardians but attended elementary school like any other children). However, emigration was seen as a particularly expedient way to deal with orphan and deserted children.

By the early twentieth century, the financial incentive first identified in the mid to late nineteenth century was overwhelming. By 31 March 1913 the average yearly cost for a Poor Law child in the metropolis was just over £26. The cheapest method was to board out the child at a cost of approximately £14; the most expensive method was to maintain children in Cottage Homes at a cost of £40 per annum. Given that children were under the care of the Board of Guardians for an average of eight years (it was often longer), then the cost to the ratepayers (for each of the 70,000 children) was £160.

Comparing this sum to the one-off payment of £20 to emigrate a child (this payment would include travelling, outfit, maintenance and inspection) it is fairly easy to see the compelling economic argument. This one-off payment would cover a child until his or her seventeenth birthday at which time they were expected to be self-sufficient. In reality, the actual cost of emigration often worked out at less than £20. For example, in 1912 the Local Government Board sanctioned the emigration to Canada of 492 orphaned or deserted children at a cost of just over £15 per child (Crane, 1915: 117). Mr Bogue Smart, the Canadian Government Inspector of British Immigrant Children reported, 'Were they available, 15,000 children per annum could be placed in comfortable homes and suitable positions.' Crane finds the savings to be made through emigration to be millions:

> The emigration of 5,000 children in the first year, at the maximum cost of £20 per child, would amount to £100,000 – a sum practically equivalent, on the estimate given above, to one year's maintenance if they were kept at home. But that would be the sole payment. Each of the five following years, until the children should have attained the School-leaving age, there would be a saving on that first batch of a like sum, or a total of £500,000. By emigrating the same number of children each of the nine following years there would be an aggregate saving to the rates of four and a half millions .... There would be a further gain by the evasion of any subsequent expense. These children, when they leave the Institution in which they have been brought up, have to battle against the stream. The industrial pressure which operates against all children of the working classes to some extent is often felt by the ex-Poor Law boy in its acutest form. (Crane, 1915: 117)

Thus, the emigration scheme would, potentially, save the local parishes millions, in the first instance alone. Given that emigration was a one-way endeavour, added to these millions would be a secondary savings in that these children would not call on the parish for support in later life – in terms of the workhouse, Casual Wards and Infirmaries. Indeed, a significant percentage of Poor Law boys were destitute before they were twenty. In addition, emigration had other significant positive benefits; it was a method of population control at a time when the population of Great Britain was increasing by three million each decade. Finally, the emigration scheme would expand the home market through empire in one further way by ensuring that the surplus labour that would be lost due to competition at home would be utilised to extend the domestic market through empire.

In summary, the forty years of the emigration of orphan and deserted children and other children is likened, by Sir John Kirk, Director of the Shaftesbury Society and the Ragged School Union as 'the saving of life ... as true and marked as that wrought by Earl Shaftesbury's factory legislation in the Victorian era'. Crane advocates in his text that 'Guardians should be urged to make greater use of their powers – which are entirely optional – to emigrate orphan and deserted children' (Crane, 1915: 133).

Forty-five years after the scheme was officially launched the emigration of orphan children of the poor was still being justified on the grounds of economics and opportunity: 'This method of dealing with such children is not only far less costly than that of keeping them at home, but also is better for the children themselves, giving them a fairer chance in life, with all its concomitants in the way of better spirits and more robust health' (Crane, 1915: vi). Doyle's allegation in 1877 that 'children are ... collected, with total disregard to fitness, physical or moral for employment [... and worse may be] unsuited for such a mode of life' (PP, 1877, LXXI, 2–3) obviously fell on fertile ground because by 1915 Crane refers to past debates in which: 'Opponents of juvenile emigration have laid stress on the fact that the overseas Dominions have been willing enough to take our best children but reluctant to take those who do not come up to a certain standard. This objection has been levelled against Canada in particular' (Crane, 1915: vii).

Thus, the warning contained in the parliamentary report of 1875 that if the complaints went unheeded and 'much greater care and discrimination ... exercised in selecting and preparing the children for emigration' then 'the whole system [... will be] brought into discredit' (PP, 1875, LXIII, 269) comes true. In 1915 Crane writes that Canada's recent 'determination to be no longer a dumping-ground for undesirables' has 'very good cause. Furthermore – and to this it is to be hoped, objectors will give due weight – Canada, even down to her Red Indians, has not stinted in giving us, in our hour of need, of her best – in troops, in armaments, in ships, in hospitals, in motor-cars, in foodstuffs and in money' (Crane, 1915: vii). Allies of war then are to reap the spoils; repayment appears to be advocated in the bodies of the best orphan children. However, proponents argued that this scheme was not to be regarded as draining England of her best orphan children for the benefit of a foreign country, but rather Canada, as a member of the Dominion should be viewed as an extension of England and thus 'those who persist in regarding her as a foreign land ... argue as if, in giving the Dominion of our best, we were making a present to some rival Power, instead of merely putting out so much capital at higher interest. Today, the solidarity of Empire has passed from the realm of rhetoric to that of actuality' (Crane, 1915: viii). Support for this viewpoint can be found in the words of Mrs Smyly from Homes in Dublin who saw her work in the emigration movement as a patriotic act: 'seeing that, ... the majority of Irish emigrants still go to the United States, this institution, whose children are sent to Canada alone, is rendering patriotic service by helping to retain emigrants within the Empire' (Crane, 1915: 40).

Crane's argument with those who persist in regarding Canada 'as a foreign land' continues the discourse of the familial configuration of the nation that I argue characterised the Victorian understanding of the state by comprising an early model of English national identity that continued through high empire into the twentieth century. What is of interest is the implicit extension of this configuration to include empire. England then was not only conceived of through a model of the family but, by extension, the empire was conceived as such – with Queen Victoria (and by implication England) acting in the role of the mother of the empire. The prosperity of the family then is linked with that of the nation and the prosperity of the empire is linked with that of Great Britain:

> If the boys can do better at home, let them stay. If they will prosper better in one of the Dominions, let them go. For what is good for the boy is finally good for the family, and, on the larger scale, what

is good for the family is good for the nation. Canada's prosperity, too, in the long run, must make for Britain's well being. (Crane, 1915: 33)

With the nation and empire being conceived of as a familial configuration, emigrating orphan children kept the resources of empire in the family in the form of inheritance. 'While by removing to Canada our warehouseman would still give another man at home a chance, he would not displace anybody overseas – unless, it might be, an alien who had designs on his inheritance' (Crane, 1915: 34). Thus, Canada (and the other dominions) acts as a provider for the state's dependent population in a familial configuration in which, 'Our overseas Dominions are to our rapidly-growing family what steady employment at better wages, and increased opportunities for his children, would be to the [impoverished labourer]' (Crane, 1915: 138). In the same way as the labourer seeks to provide for his children, 'The Government that is responsible for the children and their misfortunes, ... stands to them in the relation of parent to child' (Crane, 1915: 135). The state then would best provide for the healthy and fit orphan children by sending them out to make their fortune in the manner of a parent watching a child strike out to make a life for him or herself – this is naturalised as a rite of passage into maturity for the healthy and able-bodied. Therefore, the state should reserve its energies in supporting those who did not enjoy health and fitness and so required special attention.

Thus, emigration was not only seen as opportunity but also as character building and as a birthright – the latter which, if not protected, would be assumed by others. Crane opens *John Bull's Surplus Children* with a tale of a farmer in the 1880s who was 'of deficient energy' and suffered from 'force of circumstance'. However, the emigration to Canada and 'the bracing climate and urgent opportunities' imbue this same man with 'a certain steadiness of purpose ... He is chief executive officer of the City Council, and, among other duties, is entrusted with the care and upkeep of the civic offices, of the streets, and of the minor public works. It is not a highly remunerated position, but anything equivalent to it is status or emolument would have been beyond his reach in England' (Crane, 1915: 14).

Finally, the problem of surplus labour could be addressed by considering the empire as an internal labour market:

> The record of a man with little natural force is of itself noteworthy as showing how, by the simple transference of a citizen from one part of the Empire to another, his economic value may sometimes be improved almost beyond recognition. It also suggests the wisdom of improving facilities whereby the shortage of population and labour in some parts of this King's Dominions may be supplied from the surplus in others, instead of allowing the Englishman's birthright to pass to alien and, in some cases, inferior races. (Crane, 1915: 15)

Thus, in summary, the emigration of a 'good white stock' of orphan children not only provided them with an opportunity that for a variety of reasons would not be available in England, but also controlled the need for immigrant labour in the colonies. Such control effectively demarcated the empire as the inheritance of the English poor and ensured that the controlling face of empire was white – something which continued until the 1960s. Finally, the emigration of the orphan children to the colonies ensured a market for the expanding capitalist economy: 'Every migration converts a menace to our labour market at home into a colonial consumer of our manufactures' (Crane, 1915: 92).

Rose Macaulay's *Orphan Island* (1924) must be considered in the light of these historical records of endeavours to emigrate orphan children. Although it claims to be a narrative of the fate of one such group of fifty orphan children under the guidance of a Miss Charlotte Smith (a staunch Protestant Anglican) and two assistants (a Scottish Calvinist, Jean Fraser and a French Protestant, Anne-Marie) who were being emigrated from East London to San Francisco, it is primarily concerned with addressing debates surrounding 'Victorian values': illegitimacy, class, race and nationhood.

The tale unfolds as follows. The group of emigrants is shipwrecked during a fierce storm; only twenty orphans, Miss Smith, Jean Fraser, an intemperate Irish Catholic Dr O'Malley and four sailors survive the shipwreck marooned on a deserted island in the South Pacific. The narrative is set in 1855 – some fifteen years before the first endeavours of Miss Rye and Miss Macpherson and four years after the first emigration experiments of the St Marylebone Board of Guardians. In the staunch Anglican Miss Smith and the Scottish Calvinist Jean Fraser it is possible to identify rather ironical portraits of the two women, Miss Rye and Miss Macpherson, who started the emigration of pauper children and street 'arabs' in 1870. The second day after the shipwreck the doctor and the four sailors set out to row around the island in order to ascertain whether the island is inhabited. However, unknown to the doctor the sailors have secretly planned to attempt to row themselves, unhindered by the women and the orphan children, out to the sea so that they might be rescued. When the doctor objects to abandoning the women and children he is overcome and the sailors set off without him. He returns to the women and children and they establish a settlement. Over time he persuades the upright Miss Smith that in the eyes of the world they have been compromised so she agrees to marry him to retain her virtue, not knowing that he is already married. They have ten children and Miss Smith develops a taste for fermented drinks. However, when she discovers her drunken husband teaching his children 'popish' beliefs an argument ensues during which O'Malley tells her of their bigamous relationship and is then killed and eaten by a shark while swimming. Shocked, Charlotte reverts to her maiden name of Smith.

The narrative then jumps seventy years to Cambridge 1923 and the Thinkwell family. Mr Thinkwell, a lecturer in sociology at Cambridge is the grandson of one of the four sailors that was shipwrecked with Miss Smith. The sailors, it turns out, were rescued and Thinkwell Sr's conscience has always been plagued by his desertion of the women and children – so much so that he made a map in 1867 of where they could be found. Eventually, this letter ends up in the hands of Thinkwell Jr who decides to mount an expedition to this island, accompanied by his sons Charles (an aesthete who fought in the First World War), William (who studied natural science at Cambridge) and his daughter Rosamond (a nineteen-year-old girl who lives in the fantasy world of adventure narratives). Eventually, they find the island now populated with some two thousand descendants of the original orphans, Miss Smith and Jean Fraser. During the seventy years the island has, through the effort of Miss Smith, modelled itself on a class-based early Victorian society with Miss Smith modelling herself on Queen Victoria living in Balmoral, the Smiths and their descendants forming the land-owning class, and the orphans forming the underclass and the labouring poor. The island is rife with sectarian tensions between Protestants and Catholics (introduced by the efforts of a Jesuit priest shipwrecked at one time), between various denominations of Protestantism (the Anglicanism practised by Miss Smith and Miss Fraser's Calvinism) and racial hierarchies (as introduced by both the ethnic diversity of the orphans themselves initially and by the introduction of Africans who the Jesuit priest had been taking to exhibit in Europe when they were shipwrecked. It is these same Africans who eat the Jesuit priest).

As a birthday gesture on her ninety-eighth birthday, Miss Smith secretly grants liberty to the island's prisoners on the condition that they abscond with the rescue ships, thereby ensuring that the island's population remains imprisoned on the island. Furious at having her desire to return to Scotland denied, Miss Smith's loyal assistant, Jean Fraser, reveals to the islanders that the Smiths are all illegitimate and thus, according to the bastardy laws that they themselves passed, are ineligible to own land or hold public office. The island experiences a small revolution in which the orphan population overthrow the Smiths, the island is renamed Orphan Island (it was previously named Smith Island) and Mr Thinkwell, as a compromise to both groups becomes Prime Minister. The narrative ends with the death of Miss Smith and the introduction of reforms and new modes of thinking that enable the island to move into the twentieth century.

Although patronising, the condescending tone of the narrator helps to establish the narrative as an ironical, anthropological representation of aspects of Victorian culture. (She says, for example, 'A lady cannot, she had been well taught by her mother, discuss with a gentleman the children she and he may have, without subsequently marrying him' (Macaulay, 1924: 17); and 'The orphans were not rabbits, William' ... 'They were Victorians though (Macaulay, 1924: 29) this statement by Mr Thinkwell to his son was in reference to

Victorians' often large families'). The narrative establishes a very interesting paradigm in *Orphan Island* and raises significant issues with regards to the emigration of orphan children. First, as many accounts show, the scheme was undertaken in order to provide a better opportunity for these children than was available in England. But those contemporaries who had reservations – many of which were borne out in Doyle's report of the Rye/Macpherson scheme – are well represented in this narrative. The new world is represented as a land of opportunity but as the narrative unfolds it becomes apparent that there are also opportunities for the landowners in the New World. It is a reproduction of the class system in which the emigrated labouring and lower middle-classes find themselves as the new land-owning class. The orphans are emigrated in order to provide the labour and service the needs of this new land-owning class (paradoxically historically this was one of the objections to the emigration of orphan and poor children, i.e., they were to provide a supply of labour for the society). The scheme works on the value of the orphans as labourers; it is a scheme which confirms orphans as the exploited underclass. The orphan population, who are obliged to work for money are differentiated as belonging to the lower orders who exhibit their lowness, according to Mr Smith, 'by gesture, speech, character, and habits. Naturally there has always been a marked distinction between the descendants of my mother and the descendants of her brood of orphan children' (Macaulay, 1924: 66). Significantly, in the novel the term orphan becomes akin to class position, as demonstrated by Miss Smith's assertation that orphans comprise 'The lower and middle classes. What we call here Orphan. Troublesome people, usually. Get ideas above their station' (Macaulay, 1924: 94–5). Ultimately, one's class position is essential to one's family origins or lack thereof: 'Decidedly, Rosamond could not be Smith in her own country. She had none of the Smith outlook, but a more than Orphan commonness' (Macaulay, 1924: 82). Thus, the novel narrates orphanhood in terms of class conflict.

The narrative also works not only to establish a class hierarchy but to reinforce this hierarchy with an ethnic, racial and sectarian hierarchy as well. The narrative demonstrates Miss Smith's endeavours to establish an evangelical form of Anglicanism (often now referred to as Low Church) as the only true belief; she demonstrates a real hostility to Catholicism. Given Miss Smith's own Englishness and the representatives of Catholicism being the Irish doctor and later the French Jesuit it is fairly easy to read Anglo-Irish and Anglo-French tensions into her insistence on evangelical belief.

> She [Miss Smith] did not care for the ship's doctor, who was a papist by upbringing, an atheist by temperament, if not by conviction, a disagreeable, mocking man, a quoter of Latin tags which were probably indelicate, a lover of strong drink, and scarcely to be considered a gentleman. Miss Charlotte Smith was herself the daughter to a very respectable English country clergyman, of the Evangelical persuasion. (Macaulay, 1924: 3)

Smith's hostility to the Calvinism practised by Fraser is less intense than that displayed towards Catholicism but still present. The English–Scottish and English–Welsh tensions prevail. Finally, as almost an afterthought the marginalisation of the Jewish population is represented: 'Jews, ... were ... not well thought of on the island' (Macaulay, 1924: 210).

The orphans, with all their diverse ethnic origins 'some fifty orphans, of various nationalities and all of them under ten years of age, from East London to San Francisco' (Macaulay, 1924: 1) comprise the lower orders of this society. The ethnic diversity of the original orphans indicates that the emigration schemes were not only about emigrating poor children and orphans; but also a way to cleanse the cities and parishes from poverty and ultimately to eliminate difference. Miss Smith, who was involved in the original scheme asserts that they were: 'Orphans, picked from the gutter – no breeding among the lot of 'em. They're well enough so long as there's a firm hand over 'em' (Macaulay, 1924: 92). It must be remembered that the children were not only identified as different by their naming as 'street arabs' but that this discursively links this difference with that of the colonial subject. The narrative develops this further in the attitudes displayed by Miss Smith *et al* towards these children and through the narrator's own orientalising representations of the Polynesians in canoes – 'giggling, goggle-eyed girls and grave men'

(Macaulay, 1924: 42) – and the swarthy Mrs Albert Smith in whom a racialised identity assumes a mental deficiency: 'a large lady, very calm, very fat, and very brown, with a black moustache. She looked Spanish, for she was the daughter of a Spanish orphan, and she looked stupid, for so she was' (Macaulay, 1924: 52).

But in the colonial landscape in which the narrative is set, there is a group that exists below the lower orders – the descendants of the black African pair that the Jesuit was taking to exhibit in Europe when he was shipwrecked on the island. The Macaulays, as the black population is known, are effectively enslaved on the island as unpaid labourers – as evidenced by Mr Smith's attitude: 'No one pays the Zacharies. They don't expect it' (Macaulay, 1924: 65). In addition, the name of every black as Zachary Macaulay – ostensibly after a Scottish abolitionist – is an act which denies this group any subjectivity. It also plays on the racist assertion that 'one can never tell them apart'. The relationship between this act of naming and the author herself – Rose Macaulay – is intriguing but one into which I have not been able to make further inroads. The arrival of Aunt Adelaide Smith is the archetypal colonial image: 'She was seated in a kind of hammock, carried by two West African Negroes' (Macaulay, 1924: 64). The whole narrative moment in which the two Africans eat the Jesuit plays on colonial fears of cannibalism. The otherness of the colonised is most profoundly represented in the act of cannibalism and the coloniser constantly fears this possibility (cf., Joseph Conrad's *Heart of Darkness*). The cannibalistic act, despite the best efforts to civilise this African pair plays on fears that it is impossible to civilise all savage desires; thus the colonised are constantly expected to revert to savagery given the first opportunity as exemplified by the French Jesuit who is 'eaten up by his own Zacharies ... one day when they forgot themselves' (Macaulay, 1924: 104).

Of central importance to all of these issues is the narrative's representation of the evolution of an entire nation state from the families of the shipwrecked groups; it is a representation which makes explicit the familial nature of the nation state and the familial associations underlying class, ethnicity and national belonging, for which I have been arguing throughout this book.

And so the little island nation developed along its own lines, isolated and remote, year after year, decade after decade, century after century ... A strange community indeed! All those inter-marrying orphans of many races – what have their descendants become? And what of the descendants of the doctor and Miss Smith? What strange strands of mid-Victorian piety and prudery are woven with the primitive instincts of such a race, remote from any contacts with the wider world? (Macaulay, 1924: 19)

In *Orphan Island* then the island is simultaneously depicted as a melting pot but one in which difference is profoundly inscribed: the Zacharies have not intermixed with anyone else; a racialised spectrum is represented; there are religious dissensions and Jews are marginalised. The organisation of such a society around the central family of the descendants of the Smiths and the peripheral and marginalised descendants of the orphans' children manifests the *unheimlich* nature of the orphan figure to the family. Namely, in this setting one can identify the Smiths as the family while the orphans and their descendants embody the difference within the family. The combination of orphanhood with Irish, Scottish, Welsh and a range of other ethnicities makes explicit the link between orphanhood and notions of foreignness. This linkage highlights the racial, ethnic and sectarian tensions that exist around a constructed notion of a central Englishness comprised of racial, ethnic, religious and familial 'purity'.

This colonial outpost embodies both racial diversity and a deep-seated fear of miscegenation: the Smiths must marry amongst themselves; the entire orphan population is considered illegitimate; and the Zachary Macaulays are segregated from the general population: 'Almost from the first it was apparent that Miss Smith's children were carefully kept apart from the Orphans, trained, as it were, for a different station in life. ... They were not allowed to mix with the poor little riff-raff from East London.' (Macaulay, 1924: 175). The association of the orphans with illegitimacy develops the strong cultural association made during the Victorian time. The novel makes overt the link between orphanhood, illegitimacy and marginalisation when Marah MacBean confesses: 'We are Smith, as we said. But our mamma did not get married to our papa, so Miss Smith cast her out, and we aren't accepted in good society. We count as Orphan' (Macaulay, 1924: 82). The revelation of the illegitimacy of the entire Smith race – the ruling orders – makes explicit the profound ambivalence of the middle-class notion of family and the dark secret contained within – as was seen in my discussion of *No Name* and as will be seen in *Daniel Deronda*. The revelation of illegitimacy also subverts the Victorians' strenuous efforts to insist that the orphan children emigrated were respectable, hard working and moral poor playing on the fears and attitudes as represented by Crane. The final revelation of the illegitimacy of the whole Smith society renders their power base, according to the bastardy laws they themselves enacted, illegal. Such a revelation exposes the family, as laid claim to by the Smiths, as a constructed concept, a lie.

The fear of miscegenation is inextricably linked with a whole host of colonial attitudes and beliefs prevailing during the time; the move of the narrative to a colonial landscape which gradually becomes a colonial outpost shifts the terrain of the emigration endeavours and locates within it various colonial concerns. W.J. Moore, author of *Health in the Tropics* (1862) argued that, 'An infusion of native blood is essential to the continuance of the species, and the barrier once broken down, the remoter descendants of an European ancestor become rapidly feeble, astute, passionate, and indolent, as any of the darker races around them' (Young, 1995: 143).

The racial attitudes are revealed as the explorers anticipate finding Orphan Island and wonder about the racial composition of its present day population. Mr Merton asserts that if there is any life at all it would be most likely 'Nigger life'; and he insists that if there were any survivors then they would be a 'Lot o' half castes' because ultimately, the two races could not co-exist unmixed and even if mixed race figures did survive the standards would be 'Nigger ... Nigger always wins out. You'd find the women would sink, in one generation, to nigger notions of morality' (Macaulay, 1924: 38). This fear of miscegenation as a form of degeneration of racial 'purity' combines with the representation of the prominent Victorian belief about the degenerative effect of space (referring particularly to tropical and subtropical locations). The combination of tropical climate and the company of an intemperate Irish man causes Miss Smith to degenerate: 'she was too frequently to be found in a state of cheerful irresponsibility and garrulity very far from the discretion of her spinster days. I cannot account for this: it may have been the climate, or the influence of her husband, or merely the gradual abandonment of hope of return to the world (Macaulay, 1924: 18). This belief is epitomised in the exchange in which Mr Merton asserts that having spent such a long time on an island in the South Pacific if there were any survivors at all they would have degenerated to a 'savage' way of life.

The final gesture of 'Queen Victoria' (as played by Miss Smith) is an extremely complicated one. On one level the gesture can be read as a liberation of the island's prisoners – to return to England or wherever, a twentieth-century reverse transportation. Yet it is simultaneously an act of imprisonment of the island's population (her 'subjects') by preventing the return of the – mainly orphan – descendants to England. Is this imprisonment to be read as preventing an exodus of the colonial outpost's population to England or is it an act which symbolically plays out the reality of the emigration of the orphan scheme, that it was established as a one way ticket with little possibility of return to England? Thus, the 'imprisoning' of her subjects ensures that the orphans do not return. In this sense, Miss Smith as Queen Victoria lives on after the original is dead through the far-reaching legacy of the Victorian emigration schemes; to want to reverse the emigration schemes is seen not only as ingratitude but an act of bad faith: 'Who are you to start complaining of the good land the Lord has provided for you to live in and want to go trapesing into strange countries! You, whom we picked out of the gutter!' (Macaulay, 1924: 276). Ironically, it is Miss Smith's actions that lead to the revelation of the illegitimacy of her heirs and their rule.

Perhaps the most interesting aspect of the novel is how it grasps the complicated nature of decolonisation politics. On one level, for both the orphans and Smiths the arrival on Orphan Island signals the start of the history of Orphan Island. The inhabitants themselves refer to the shipwreck on the island as: 'the beginning of our history, when our grandparents came over' (Macaulay, 1924: 49). It is an absolute colonial move; history starts with colonisation by the West, any other existence is relegated to prehistory. On another level, the inhabitants of Orphan Island identify themselves with a double subjectivity: that of the rooted and established inhabitants of Orphan Island and as subjects to Great Britain. Their response to the question of repatriation to Great Britain is one which recognises their centre as both Orphan Island and Great Britain.

> You seem to be proposing, my dear young gentleman, a complete emigration of our population to some other country. A little wholesale, surely. We have, you see, our roots, our family and national life, our means of livelihood, our history and traditions, here on this island, which I observe that you describe as 'desert'. Of course we know, for we have always been taught so here, that Great Britain, the country from which we originally emigrated, and which you now inhabit, is the world's hub, peculiarly chosen by the Deity as the centre of His beneficent purposes towards the universe. We have ... taken Great Britain, her constitution, her customs and the unrivalled purity of her domestic and social life, for our model in this island colony. (Macaulay, 1924: 57)

However, it is the insistence on their own independence within the realm of empire that demonstrates that they have a notion of being both part of the imagined community of Great Britain through empire and of Orphan Island as evidenced in Mrs Smith's assertion: 'But we are an independent community, I may say a *principality*, and we have, I think, no desire permanently and as a nation to abandon our island home' (Macaulay, 1924: 57). Miss Smith's subsequent questioning of the offer of repatriation can be seen as twofold: a questioning of the idea of returning to a home (Great Britain) which is no longer a home; and a querying of the premise and enthusiasm for the emigration schemes which resulted in the arrival of their forefathers at Orphan Island. 'Why should the whole population of this island suddenly take it into their heads to emigrate? Does the whole population of Great Britain desire to leave it? ... The Orphans are very well as they are. Let 'em be, and don't go putting notions into their heads' (Macaulay, 1924: 91). The novel appears to suggest that the work of settlement, like the emigration schemes is a one-way affair: the process is transformative; the emigrants are immutably changed in the process and no return is possible. The narrator argues: 'Here, after all, they had a living; here was the land they knew, and, if its existing order should be changed and bettered, so that all had their fair share, it might be best to stay on it' (Macaulay, 1924: 316).

Yet despite the complicated nature of belonging on the part of the inhabitants of Orphan Island, it is still represented very much in terms of a dependent colonial outpost which relies on the civil structures and cultural discourses of Great Britain for intellectual and political leadership. The revolutionary uprising of the 'vociferous crowd of orphans' (Macaulay, 1924: 304) which promises so much resonates with similar uprisings in Ireland at the time. (The identification of the political writing – a revolutionary poem – written by a Michael Connolly in 1910 which began – 'Orphans, arise! throw off the tyrants' yoke,' and ended – 'To that great day when Smith shall be no more' (Macaulay, 1924: 254) and the agitation in the newspapers to 'take the island from these so-called Smiths!' (Macaulay, 1924: 282) could refer to the issue of British colonialism in Ireland or equally to the Dublin Tram lockout of 1913. However, the significance of a revolutionary cry first voiced in a poem by a man of Irish descent resonates with the involvement of Irish literary figures in the decolonisation movement.) The representation of the orphans as revolutionary proletarians and the Smiths (colonisers) as fascist (Thinkwell notices a remarkable similarity between Mr Smith's censuring of the press and Mussolini in Italy (Macaulay, 1924: 77)) suggests a link between colonialism and fascism – a link which is first developed by Aime Césaire in *Discourse on Colonialism* and later by Albert Memmi in *The Colonizer and the Colonized*. However, ultimately the narrative shies away from such a radical stance; the revolutionary fervour of the orphans only in fact paves the way for a Cambridge academic to bring the island into the twentieth century: 'The island – Orphan Island now, by government proclamation – settled down. The newly-constituted parliament, under the thoughtful, just, and moderating guidance of Mr Thinkwell, got to work on the amendation of the laws of the land and the readjust-ment of property' (Macaulay, 1924: 317). Thus, Cambridge as a home of great minds plays a progressive and civilising influence in late colonial times:

> The island underwent – is now undergoing – an intellectual as well
> as a political renaissance. It is producing, for good or ill, a considerable body of indifferent literature and art. It also has a flourishing
> drama and stage. Learning in all branches has been extended and
> reinforced by the stock of it introduced by the Cambridge
> Thinkwells. William has been made Instructor in Science, and
> twentieth century views of the cosmos have supervened on the
> dying and despised Paleyology imparted by Miss Smith.
> (Macaulay, 1924: 320)

It is a response to one of the contemporary problems faced: how to bring colonial enclaves still effectively living in the Victorian age into the twentieth century while still maintaining colonial control? The narrative offers us the figure of Mr Thinkwell as an enlightened colonial administrator as a solution.

The fundamental question remains that posed by the narrator: 'Will the Orphans, leaving their newly constituted republic and their now more prosperous homes, lightly adventure in unknown lands?' (Macaulay, 1924: 322). In representing the draw of the centre of empire, the mother country, to the emigrant population in the colonies the narrative demonstrates how one can hold loyalties to both the country of familial origin and the country of habitation – the paradoxical affiliation of the immigrant calms fears that England will be swamped by hoards of colonial subjects (children) only waiting for a chance to reverse the one way ticket and return to the land of their familial origin.

> It is certain that Flora and Heathcliff and Peter, and many others of
> the young and adventurous, will take any opportunity they may get
> to see the world, as they call Great Britain. But it is by no means so
> certain that, should they ever see it, they would remain in it long.
> Why should they? It is cold; it rains; it has large towns; its vegetation
> is poor, its sea poorer. It has, in short, few advantages over Orphan
> Island, beyond mere novelty and size. (Macaulay, 1924: 322)

Part of the way of constructing the draw of the new homeland is to revert to the colonial stereotype of the colonies as Edenic and prelapsarian – an ideal, naturalised existence that is out of history. This is seen as a fitting birthright for children constructed as innocent, 'unspotted by the world' (Macaulay, 1924: 89). However, in the narrative of progress and development, history ultimately encroaches, 'Though even here [according to Miss Smith] sin has crept in, like the serpent into Eden' (Macaulay, 1924: 89).

Finally, what is of most relevance to the emigration schemes is the fact that what is offered as a birthright and a new opportunity for those orphans that cannot be supported in England in fact replicates the same social configuration that worked to oppress them there. As time passes on Orphan Island, the orphans as labourers cultivate the land while the Smiths own all the land. It is a fact not lost on the Thinkwells: 'It strikes me that all the European vices and imbecilities thrive on Orphan Island. First a few of them steal the land from the many, then they spoil it. I hate these Smiths' (Macaulay, 1924: 190). So, in fact, the land of opportunity is no more than an extension of the social structures of home.

5

Exile and return

> The experience of colonizing did not leave the internal culture of
> Britain untouched. It began to bring into prominence those parts of
> the British political culture which were least tender and humane.
> ... It openly sanctified – in the name of such values as competition,
> achievement, control and productivity – new forms of institutional-
> ized violence and social Darwinism. ... The tragedy of colonialism
> was also the tragedy of the younger sons, the women, and all 'the
> etceteras and-so-forths' of Britain. (Nandy, 1983: 32)

TO THE EXTENT that family, nation and empire were all
inextricably interrelated, it stands to reason that, as
Nandy intimates in *The Intimate Enemy*, the experience
of empire-building profoundly affected not only the family – as has
been argued in the previous chapters – but also the nation and
discourses of national identity. New discourses of cosmopolitanism
contested older nationalistic discourses as the constituent population
of England, more specifically London, started to diversify with an
influx from the colonies and other parts of the world. This chapter
examines the extent to which discourses of orphanhood conflate with
those of ethnic difference in the latter part of the century. To do this
I will be examining two specific texts – *Daniel Deronda* and *The
Mystery of Edwin Drood* – in order to analyse how both Eliot and
Dickens conceive of the ethnic difference present in London and the
surrounding areas. For Eliot, the cosmopolitanism borne of empire
threatens notions of English nationalism. She looked to the difference within – embodied in the figure of the Jew and the Jewish
community – to offer a model of nationalism to which England could

aspire. Dickens, on the other hand, looked to the return of British subjects from the colonies in order to explore notions of racial difference and the impact of the East on the heart of empire.

> Eliot uses the plight of Jews to make a universal statement about the nineteenth century's need for a home, given the spiritual and psychological rootlessness reflected in her characters' almost ontological physical restlessness. Her interest in Zionism therefore can be traced to the reflection, made early in the novel, that ... To find the 'early home' means to find the place where originally one was at home ... It becomes historically appropriate therefore that those individuals and that 'people' best suited to the task are Jews. Only the Jews as a people (and consequently as individuals) have retained both a sense of their original home in Zion and an acute, always contemporary, feeling of loss. (Said, 1979, 19)

In returning once more to the quotation from *Daniel Deronda* which opened this book, it is now possible to read the narrator's meditation on the importance of home and rootedness in the same light as Froude's writings: a melancholia for a familial, and national unity. But in this particular case, the melancholia is not only a response to the imperial context abroad but is a response to the increasing cosmopolitanism and fragmentation within England: the heart of empire. Such cosmopolitanism posed a threat to the composition of national belonging; melancholia was the structure which objectified the familial and national ideals and through which one could mourn their disappearance.

Eliot shares the same views expressed, both implicitly and explicitly, in all of the texts considered: namely, that at the heart of nation lies the home and the family. This family structure reproduces itself through a process of inheritance which constitutes not only material wealth but name, social place and familial tradition/practices. Eliot envisaged the nation working in the same way – firmly rooted in the past and providing an inheritance of cultural values and traditions for its children. The children, for their part, were then obliged to honour the 'parents', e.g., the nation. This is the view put forth by Bernard Semmel in *George Eliot and the Politics of Inheritance*:

The life of the individual could not be separated from that of the nation, whose past had shaped him and to whose traditions he was the heir, regardless of his own wishes. Duties replace rights in Eliot's vision, and those duties find their place primarily in the family and in the national community as an extended family. Parents had the duty not only to pass on their goods to their children but also to nurture their offspring; and children had filial obligations to nurturing parents. The nation – with its rich traditions and culture – was such a nurturing parent. (Semmel, 1994: 13)[16]

Eliot's attraction to the past should be read within contemporary debates about nationalism versus cosmopolitanism. In valourising the importance of past and tradition Eliot pits herself against notions of the cosmopolitan and aligns herself with a number of nationalist thinkers, e.g., Comte, Herder, Hegel, Coleridge and John Stuart Mill (Semmel, 1994: 14). Edmund Burke is one of the clearest influences on Eliot *vis-à-vis* the past and the notion of national inheritance. For Burke, the essence of English liberty is 'as an entailed inheritance derived to us from our forefathers, and to be transmitted to our posterity – as an estate belonging to the people of this kingdom ... [Thus England can be seen to be comprised of] an inheritable crown, an inheritable peerage, and a House of Commons and a people inheriting privileges, franchises and liberties from a long line of ancestors' (Burke, 1955: 28–9). Burke, like others at the time, argued for the familial structure of the nation and a dated notion of nationalism in the face of both increasing fragmentation and discourses of cosmopolitanism. Eliot herself argues for an 'analogous relation' between individual morality and the 'social conditions they have inherited' when she firmly identifies the roots of one's nature as being 'intertwined with the past, and ... developed by allowing those roots to remain undisturbed while the process of development is going on' (Eliot, 1963: 289–90).

Such then is the context that Said grasps in the opening quote: the desperate assertion of, or even search for, an originary notion of home that not only gives one a personal and familial identity, but acts as the single originary moment which binds both a community and a nation of like people together. It is a melancholic notion of collective roots and rootedness.[17] Eliot enacts these debates within the novel in a discussion between Mordecai and Pash. Pash argues that 'the sentiment' of nationality is a backward idea which is 'destined to die out' as the 'whole current of progress is against it'. Mordecai responds that 'the soul of Judaism is not dead'; Mordecai argues for the 'unity of Israel' founded in its religion becoming 'an outward reality. Looking towards a land and a polity, our dispersed people in all the ends of the earth may share the dignity of a national life which has a voice among the peoples of the East and the West' (Eliot, 1984: 584–92). As the narrative sympathy lies in general with Mordecai's view rather than that of Pash, one can see how the novel sides with the nationalists' aspirations.

With the focus on an originary moment and the consequent melancholia for a lost home/nation, Eliot turns to the Jewish community for a model of how such a 'nation' continues to function. Four years after writing *Daniel Deronda*, Eliot celebrates the Jew and the Jewish community in 'The Modern Hep! Hep! Hep!' both as a model for a fragmented English nation in danger of becoming completely dissociated from a notion of the nation's past and 'for his preservation of good qualities despite the persecution that might have left him bereft of them, as well as for the special role Judaism had played in the development of Christian civilization' (Eliot, 1925: 261). For Eliot, the Jewish community remains united by the collective perception of an originary homeland; this perception gives this community, in Eliot's view, a historical authenticity. For the critics who, unlike F.R. Leavis (Leavis, 1949: 79–125), take the 'Jewish' plot as worthy of consideration this is an identifiable strand in the critical perception of how Eliot conceives the Jew. Irving Howe argues that in the Jewish community Eliot identified a 'barely-dawning movement of the Jews toward national regroupment ... that might arouse the imagination of cultivated modern people'. In other words Eliot identified a foundling nationalism that would offer 'a usable symbol for the search, ... for modes of action through which to realise moral ideas' (Howe, 1979: 363–4). The crux of Howe's argument is that Jewish national aspirations could revitalise English national identity.

The figure of the Jew offers Eliot an ethical figure in a world of 'godlessness'; Jewish tradition offers a moral grounding for all religious life (Howe, 1979: 361). Lisbeth During picks up on the notion of a moral locus when she argues:

> The ethic Eliot has in mind has grown too large, too unwieldy and speculative for the terms of 'Britishness' ... it is an Hebraic ethic of history, responsibility, prophecy, transcendence.
>
> The moral conception which reflected the conditions and values of the eighteenth-century British aristocracy could not respond to the dilemmas of a nineteenth century community, uneasy with its traditional deferences, a community which had seen the erosions of modernity and the economic instability of most traditional institutions. (During, 1993: 107–8)

One of the main tenets of During's argument then is that Eliot offers 'an indictment of the failings of English culture' by using the model of 'the imaginary nation' of the Jewish diaspora that 'puts into practice the ethic which English society can no longer live up to' (During, 1993: 108). This line of argument can be identified in Semmel's work as well where he argues for the figure of the Jew as the superego: 'Jews came to represent conscience, moral judges who might on occasion be unpleasantly censorious: if the Gypsy and the Christian were the id, the Jew was the superego ... The opening scene of *Daniel Deronda* pictures Daniel, raised as an English gentleman ignorant of his Jewish origins, exercising the same moral authority as Sephardo had' (Semmel, 1994: 121). These readings are borne out by the representation of Daniel as priest and prophet in the text. Daniel first functions as a priest and confessor figure to Gwendolen and it is to him she looks for guidance on how to live an ethical way of life (Eliot, 1984: 673, 754). Then Daniel functions as a prophet to the larger Jewish community itself. Daniel's early life is seen by the community as part of the process by which 'the erring and unloving wills of men' have helped to prepare him 'as Moses was prepared, to serve ... [his] people the better (Eliot, 1984: 818). Significantly, the priesthood, as defined by Gwendolen and the largely secular Christian community is something Daniel ultimately shrinks from and rebukes (Eliot, 1984: 754), while the role of prophet for the

Jewish community is a role which Daniel embraces both from a sense of love and duty – the very qualities which Eliot believes familial/ national inheritance should inspire.

However, the primary concern of this chapter is not so much the representation of the figure of the Jew in the novel but how Eliot consciously conflates orphanhood with the Jewish condition. Daniel laments not having the 'sharp duty' that comes with birthright. As an orphan, outside the legitimate family, Daniel is without both filial obligations and familial inheritance – the latter which would give him a family name, social place, home – all the aspects of a familial identity. As an orphan, Daniel lacks the certainty that even Mirah has in her remembrance of her early life of 'waking up and loving my mother's face: it was so near to me, and her arms were round me, and she sang to me' (Eliot, 1984: 250). Even though Mirah has lost her mother her familial and cultural identity is known and intact. For Daniel, the concept of parents exists as an imaginary/lost concept: 'To Daniel the words Father and Mother had the altar-fire in them; and the thought of all closest relations of our nature held still something of the mystic power which had made his neck and ears burn in boyhood' (Eliot, 1984: 526). This loss forms the basis of his melancholia. Daniel mourns the loss of his parents whose influence would

> Justify partiality, and making him what he longed to be yet was unable to make himself – an organic part of social life, instead of roaming in it like a yearning, disembodied spirit, stirred with a vague social passion, but without fixed local habitation to render fellowship real? … He found some of the fault in his birth and the way he had been brought up, which had laid no special demands on him and given him no fixed relationships except one of a doubtful kind. (Eliot, 1984: 413–14)

Daniel lacks the rootedness ('fixed location') and community (organic social life) that comes from the community of blood relations cele- brated by the narrator in the quote which opened this book. Instead Daniel exists as a 'disembodied spirit', melancholic for a notion of family and homeland. The paradox of his lack of rootedness is that he has been brought up in a respected and influential family; he is perceived in many ways as the archetypal English gentlemen. With all his aristocratic trappings Daniel is, in some aspects, an insider. Yet difference exists within the very bosom of this notional family; Daniel is both of the family and not of the family – as later he will be seen as both Christian and Jew. This hybrid identity, of being both insider and outsider, is one which Daniel cannot sustain – he feels alienated within his adopted family/nation, within the very structure which 'laid no special demands on him' and which gave him 'no fixed relationships except one of a doubtful kind'. Daniel's alienation from the familial structure and inheritance is well understood in the community as is epitomised by the comments of one of Mallinger's guests, 'Well, of course he is under some disadvantage: it is not as if he were Lady Mallinger's son. He does not inherit the property, and he is not of any consequence in the world' (Eliot, 1984: 379). Daniel himself keenly feels his alienation through his lack of inheritance as 'a secret hardship ... that any circumstances of his birth had shut him out from the inheritance of his father's position' (Eliot, 1984: 476). The notions of disembodiment combined with the lack of an organic social life and fixed home suggest Daniel be read as in exile – the lost family for which he yearns is synonymous with the notion of an originary homeland. It is a linkage which Eliot suggests in the novel when Daniel sits in the synagogue and 'saw faces there probably little different from those of his grandfather's time, and heard the Spanish–Hebrew liturgy which had lasted through the seasons of wandering generations like a plant with a wandering seed, that give the far-off lands a kinship to the exile's home' (Eliot, 1984: 748). Ultimately, Daniel finds a sense of originary familial and national identity when he discovers his Jewish roots. It is to this family/nation that Daniel devotes the rest of his life in obedient filial duty. The irony in this final revelation of his familial identity is that it, in effect, confirms his feelings of alienation within England and his adopted family: discovering his familial origin makes Daniel a permanent outsider to the larger community and an insider to the Jewish community.

Thus, orphanhood comes to signify (ethnic) difference within the novel. Daniel's difference is signalled from the onset of the novel when he stands in the portrait gallery of his supposed relatives. The

narrative is careful to establish that 'in the nephew Daniel Deronda
the family faces of various types, seen on the walls of the gallery,
found no reflex' (Eliot, 1984: 205). As the narrative progresses, the
nature of this singular difference becomes racialised as people speculate 'without being told, that there was foreign blood in his veins'
(Eliot, 1984: 378). This same mark of difference which distinguishes
Deronda from those around him is precisely the same mark by which
his origins 'will out'; he is continually interpellated by members of
the Jewish community as Jewish (Eliot, 1984: 417, 437, 559, 633–4).
In the revelation of his parentage, Eliot adopts the same discourse of
racial purity that permeates the novel when she creates a genealogy
for Daniel that is a direct pure learned line from an originary form of
Judaism; Daniel's inheritance is the documents which will enable
him to provide the link between his contemporary Jewish community
and the past. 'It is not only that I am a Jew ... but I come of a strain
that has ardently maintained the fellowship of our race – a line of
Spanish Jews that has borne many students and men of practical
power. And I possess what will give us a sort of communion with
them' (Eliot, 1984: 817). It is not enough then that Daniel has Jewish
roots but Eliot ensures that these roots are special, unique – a Jewish
equivalent to the aristocratic position that he has been brought up to
enjoy. The difference between Eliot's representation of the noble
Jewish characters in the novel and the Jewish characters from the
lower classes is striking. Take the portraits of Mr Cohen and some of
the other shopkeepers, for example where the discourse of purity is
contrasted with that of mongrelism:

> Mr Cohen's aspect ... showed that tendency to look mongrel
> without due cause which, in a miscellaneous London neighbour-
> hood, may perhaps be compared with the marvels of imitation in
> insects, and may have nature's imperfect effort on behalf of the
> purer Caucasian to shield him from the shame and spitting to
> which purer features would have been exposed in the times of zeal.
> Mr Ram dealt ably in books in the same way that he would have
> dealt in tins of meat and other commodities – without knowledge
> or responsibility as to the proportion of rottenness or nourishment
> they might contain. (Eliot, 1984: 562)

Both portraits contain the paradoxical workings of orientalism – the exalted exotic and the undesirable oriental (Said, 1978). Mr Ram's indifferent ignorance is a notable contrast to Daniel and Mordecai's learning and thirst for knowledge. The revelation of a wealthy and distinguished family origin is a key element to the orphan popular narratives discussed in previous chapters and is something to which I will return.

Finding his mother not only provides Daniel with the certainty of lineage, familial and cultural identity, and the corresponding inheritance, but simultaneously re-orphans Daniel as his mother casts him off once again: the royalty to which Daniel's mother lays claim has no genealogy ('A great singer and actress is a queen, but she gives no royalty to her son' (Eliot, 1984: 697)). In re-orphaning Daniel, the Princess refuses the role demanded of her both by her religion and by virtue of her gender: namely to act as the repository and transmitter of the cultural values that are a crucial component of her child's identity. Likewise, Daniel's desire to fulfil his filial duty to his mother is repulsed, 'The moment was cruel: it made the filial yearning of his life a disappointed pilgrimage to a shrine where there were no longer the symbols of sacredness' (Eliot, 1984: 723–4), but his inheritance – in the form of the trunk of documents that definitively traces and inscribes his ancestral past – gives him not only a cultural identity and community but a responsibility to this cultural community and its endeavours. For the first time, Daniel possesses a sense of certitude and belonging; he pledges his 'service' and his 'duty' to his 'people' (Eliot, 1984: 725). In discovering his ancestry Daniel finds 'an added soul' and a 'noble partiality' with which he has affiliation (Eliot, 1984: 814).

> He beheld the world changed for him by certitude of ties that altered the poise of hopes and fears, and gave him a new sense of fellowship, as if under cover of the night he had joined the wrong band of wanderers, and found with the rise of morning that the tents of his kindred were grouped far off. He had a quivering imaginative sense of close relation to the grandfather who had been animated by strong impulses and beloved thoughts, which were now perhaps being roused from their slumber within himself.
> (Eliot, 1984: 747)

Thus, paradoxically, it is through the male line, in the figures of his maternal grandfather and Mordecai, that Daniel is able to realise aspects of his familial and communal identity. However, although his mother refuses her maternal role, it is through meeting her that he comes to know his genealogy, thus nullifying the spectres of illegitimacy and miscegenation that operate so powerfully in the orphan narratives. Instead, Daniel's new-found familial genealogy also gives him a place in the Jewish community and in the nation-building project. It is a revelation that confers a belonging that operates throughout the popular orphan adventure narrative: the discovery of one's genealogy restores the orphan to his community and social status.

One form which Daniel's pledge of service and duty to his people takes is the fulfilment of the Zionist project to establish a Jewish homeland in land that was occupied by the Palestinian population. In this moment the strands concerning family, community, nationalism and homeland conflate within an imperial discourse. Once again the figure of the orphan is the vehicle through which this imperialism is expressed but the effects of the imperial project in the novel are twofold. First, in terms of the project as a colonising mission, Eliot was careful to distinguish such imperialism from nationalism in her rejection of the moral validity of colonisation while preserving a place for nationalism. 'While England had no right to impose its political rule or culture on other nations, it ought to resist the liberal view that decried national feeling as outgrown barbarism' (Eliot, 1925: 265–6).

Yet, despite her stated opposition to the colonial mission, Eliot still celebrates Daniel's new found duty and mission to do just that. Daniel embraces the Zionist project to establish a Jewish settlement on land occupied by the Palestinians; far from being condemned his representation in the text is akin to that of a prophet. In fact, in conceiving a Jewish state to act as a buffer between the civilised West and the 'despotic' East, one can, as Susan Meyer has argued, identify how this state would help British interests in the Middle East, especially *vis-à-vis* difficulties with Syria at the time (cf., Susan Meyer, 1993: 773–858). However, Eliot's contradictory stance does not end there. It is perhaps ironic that, given that the Jewish community is celebrated as a model of blood relations and organic nationalism rooted in history to which Eliot feels implicitly Britain should aspire, the future for such a community is not to be found in Britain; its uniqueness excludes it from any model of British nationalism. More specifically, once Daniel's Jewish roots are revealed his alienation from the family/community/nation of Britain is complete; there is no immediate future or place for him in Britain, he must, in his own words, leave Britain in order to find belonging.

> I am going East to become better acquainted with the condition of my race in various countries there . . . . The idea that I am possessed with is that of restoring a political existence to my people, making them a nation again, giving them a national centre, such as the English have, though they are too scattered over the face of the globe. That is a task which presents itself to me as a duty: I am resolved to begin it, however feebly. I am resolved to devote my life to it. At the least I may awaken a movement in other minds, such as has been awakened in my own. (Eliot, 1984: 875)

The effects of an imperialistic endeavour such as Britain has undertaken by this time are actually seen as causes for the breakdown of a sense of rooted community. Froude's writing from the colonies reveal a melancholic loss of a notion of family, home, community and nation. For Britain imperialism, rather than giving it the national centre that Deronda perceives, has in fact, scattered the population throughout the world in the British colonies. So, on one hand, as Carolyn Lesjak has persuasively argued (Lesjak, 1996: 40), the fledgling Zionist project to which Deronda pledges himself works in conjunction with current British imperial aspirations and capitalist endeavours, while, on the other, British imperialism is perceived to be causing the disintegration of the rooted sense of family/community that Eliot sees as vital to a British national identity. This disintegration is brought about both through a weakening or even severing of the link between England, its past, and the Anglo communities living in the colonies (an English imperial diaspora in Eliot's mind?), and through the introduction of an increased cosmopolitanism to the centre of empire, London. So in the final analysis Eliot chooses to locate the horrors of imperialism within Britain itself and not in the colonies. She tries to reconcile the effects of such imperialism and loss of community in the hybrid figure of Deronda who is at once both English and Jewish. 'The effect of my education can never be done away with. The Christian sympathies in which my mind was reared can never die out of me ... But I consider it my duty – it is the impulse of my feeling – to identify myself, as far as possible, with my hereditary people' (Eliot, 1984: 724).

In this figure, Eliot shows how one recovers a lost identity and a lost link with the past and how one is reintegrated within a community. In Deronda's search for a homeland elsewhere we find the reverse of what Eliot might be advocating: in her aversion to imperialism one can identify a possible cause of the loss of an English community. Thus, the solution is that advocated by Deronda – a return to the originary homeland and the (re)establishment of a rooted national identity. However, in keeping with the very imperialist agenda that Eliot appears to criticise, Deronda, as Said argues (Said, 1979), needs his own colonising mission as there is no place for his national aspirations within England.

The metaphor of exile, whether in the colonies or abroad, is also a particularly powerful one in dealing with middle-class orphans: in addition to Deronda one need only think of Pip in *Great Expectations* (Dickens, 1987) or Lucy Snowe in *Villette* (C. Brontë, 1991). Lucy can be read an outcast; one who by her own admission takes her place in her own narrative in 'the outer ranks of the crowd ... [which was] made up of citizens, plebeians and police' (Brontë, 1991: 564). The cultural and linguistic alienation which she experiences in Brussels symbolises how her orphanhood places her outside the signifying practices of language and culture and doubles her alienation.

What seems to be happening in *Daniel Deronda* then, is that while Eliot critiques imperialism and attempts to separate it from national identity, she ignores the fact that, as Lesjak argues, at this particular historical juncture nationalism and imperialism were working in conjunction with one another (Lesjak, 1996: 38). As has been argued earlier in the book, one obvious way in which the two worked together was in the popular orphan adventure narratives. In many ways *Daniel Deronda* is structured in a very similar way to these narratives. One of the key elements in these narratives is the deprivation of heritage that the orphan suffers as a result of his/her orphanhood. In the middle-class narratives, this deprivation takes the form of a loss of the inheritance of name, social wealth and position. Semmel talks very usefully of *Daniel Deronda* being read as 'the myth of the disinherited one .... The novel's plot includes a romantic search for a father, an identity, and a mission, ... the hidden token of their birth and its inheritance of tasks' (Semmel, 1994: 18–19). Thus, Daniel heads off to the East as part of his mission of establishing a Jewish homeland. But the East to which Daniel travels can be seen as contained within the West: an 'orientalised' construct of Western imagination (Said, 1978).

In the working-class narratives, however, this disinheritance was a result of these orphans being orientalised as the embodiment of an absolute, foreign difference within Victorian culture. This disinheritance translated into a loss of homeland as many of these orphans were forced to leave England, for the colonies or the merchant navy. In *The Mystery of Edwin Drood* the Landlesses return from the East – in the form of their 'home' in the colonies – in search of social place/homeland in England. *The Mystery of Edwin Drood* works in reverse then to *Daniel Deronda*: in the orphan figure's return to England in search of a homeland we have come full circle. As such, this text marks the first of a number of popular orphan adventure narratives in which the orphan returns to England.

Like Eliot, Dickens had a long standing interest in the impact of the peripheries of empire on the domestic life of the metropolis; the interest is discernible as early as *Oliver Twist* in Monk's influence on Oliver's familial inheritance, through *Dombey and Son*,[18] *David Copperfield* (the fates of L'il Emily and Peggotty), *Bleak House* (where the interests in doing good for those in faraway lands causes one's own children to be neglected), and *Great Expectations*. However, in *The Mystery of Edwin Drood*, Dickens's interest lay in the effect of racialised British subjects and empire on the heart of England. More specifically, in *The Mystery of Edwin Drood*,

Dickens's exploration of views on race and ethnicity can be read in conjunction with his other writings on race. Dickens's first writings on the subject during the Indian Mutiny were explored in Chapter 3.

After 1857, Dickens continued to offer outspoken views on the treatment of people of other races. In 1865 he publicly supported Governor Eyre's brutal actions to 'put down' the Morant Bay rebellion. Indeed *The Mystery of Edwin Drood* contains veiled references to the public debates around Eyre's actions, reiterating Dickens's support for 'strong' rule. Dickens offers, in Mr Honeythunder, a scathing portrait of the philanthropists who spoke on the platform against Governor Eyre. By identifying this philanthropy as the 'gunpowderous sort' which in reality was no different from 'animosity', Dickens reveals his own hostility. Honeythunder's speech, therefore, is highly ironical: 'You were to abolish military force, but you were first to bring all commanding officers who had done their duty, to trial by court martial for that offence, and shoot them. ... Above all things you were to do nothing in private or on your own account. You were to go to the offices of the Haven of Philanthropy ... and were ever more to live upon the platform' (Dickens, 1989: 57–8). In a letter in 1868, after his 1867–68 tour of America, Dickens is scathing about the possibility of extending the suffrage to black Americans: 'The melancholy absurdity of giving these people votes ... would glare at one out of every roll of their eyes, chuckle of their mouths, and bump in their heads, if one did not see ... that their enfranchisement is a mere party trick to get votes' (Dickens, 1938: 3, 618).

What is of interest then in *The Mystery of Edwin Drood* is not so much Dickens's views on race *per se*, rather the fact that empire and its contact with people of other races is seen ultimately as a contagion which infects even the heart of the 'sweet-voiced choir', the choirmaster, of an old English cathedral town. Dickens establishes this contagion from the opening of the novel in a scene where Jasper in an opium haze hallucinates:

> What is the spike that intervenes, and who has set it up? Maybe it
> is set up by the Sultan's orders for the impaling of a horde of
> Turkish robbers, one by one. It is so, for cymbals clash, and the

Sultan goes by to his palace in long procession. Ten thousand scimitars flash in the sunlight, and thrice ten thousand dancing-girls strew flowers. Then, follow white elephants caparisoned in countless gorgeous colours, and infinite in number and attendants. Still the Cathedral Tower rises in the background, where it cannot be, and still no writhing figure is on the grim spike. (Dickens, 1989: 1)

The orphans in question then are Britains born abroad who possess a 'mixture of oriental blood – or imperceptibly acquired nature in them' (Stone, 1987: 385). Indeed, as Suvendrini Perera argues, in *The Mystery of Edwin Drood* Dickens writes 'the narrative of a civilization contaminated by eastern savagery (Perera, 1991: 108).

In *The Mystery of Edwin Drood* there is a certain unknown element to the parentage of the two orphan Landless twins – their name reveals as much. This unknown element invites speculation, and the spectre of miscegenation, not illegitimacy, haunts the twins. In addition to the lack of a known genealogy, the Landless twins are just that, since they are homeless. Born in the former Ceylon (Sri Lanka) to at least one British parent, the twins are without a discernible homeland; they have little claim to kinship, blood relations, community or nation. Their possible mixed race embodies their foreignness and lack of belonging in both the colonial community and in England; it is a mark of difference which, through a lack of a discernible genealogy, conflates with orphanhood as Deronda's ethnic identity does. In Ceylon, the orphans are treated like slaves: they had a 'wretched existence' under a guardian 'who grudged us food to eat and clothes to wear.' When their guardian dies they are passed capriciously, like possessions, not to any close friend but to a man 'whose name was always in print and catching his attention' (Dickens, 1989: 60). It is important to note that however badly the twins were treated they, or more specifically Neville, still had the power and authority to cause 'sundry natives' to be whipped to death (Dickens, 1989: 198). While in England, the orphan twins are ostracised: unlike Deronda's hybrid identity, the hybridity of the Landless twins leaves them in an ambivalent position as nomadic wanderers with a claim to British subject status yet profoundly alienated within the British community. As with other popular orphan adventure narratives of the time the return to England from the colonies proves a difficult one; Britain is unwelcoming to returning subjects.

Hence, from their arrival in Cloisterham, the Landless twins are established as foreign others. The earliest descriptions of them dwell on the marks of their racial difference – associating them with the East, dangerous animals of the East, and the gypsy population.

> An unusually handsome lithe young fellow, and an unusually hand-some lithe girl; much alike; both very dark, and very rich in colour; she of almost the gipsy type; something untamed about them both; a certain air upon them of hunter and huntress; yet withal a certain air of being the objects of the chase, rather than the followers. Slender, supple, quick of eye and limb; half shy, half defiant; fierce of look; an indefinable kind of pause coming and going on their whole expression, both of face, and form, which might be equally likened to the pause before a crouch or a bound. (Dickens, 1989: 56–7)

In fact, Crisparkle's own musings about the Landlesses reveals how he has been influenced by imperial tales of exotic places in that 'he wondered ... much if they were beautiful barbaric captives brought from some wild tropical dominion' (Dickens, 1989: 57). Not only do they find themselves unwelcome in society but Neville is very quickly accused of a heinous crime; as a result he is 'shunned ... and cast ... out' (Dickens, 1989: 187). But because of their mark of other-ness perhaps the real crime being alluded to is their foreignness. This is further supported when Edwin Drood incites Neville to uncon-trollable fury in implying that because of his own racial genealogy he has no place in white society.

> 'How should you know? You may know a black common fellow, or a black common boaster, when you seen him (and no doubt you have a large acquaintance that way); but you are no judge of white men.'
>
> This insulting allusion to his dark skin infuriates Neville to that violent degree, that he flings the dregs of his wine at Edwin Drood, and is in the act of flinging the goblet after it, when his arm is caught in the nick of time by Jasper. (Dickens, 1989: 76)

The Landlesses are unassimilable because of their racialised identity. In fact, Sapsea forms the basis of his presumption of Neville's guilt on the fact that his complexion is 'un-English' (Dickens, 1989: 164). The lack of known parentage translates into a lack of rootedness in England; indeed their plan is to quickly rid themselves of their appointed guardian and wander through the country. It is significant that the early descriptions of the twins' telepathy emphasises their possession of the power, and with this the assumed violence, of the East.

It is interesting to note, however, that the narrative delineates the two twins in a very complex manner: they are not simply demonised. In their portraits it is possible to identify the pendulum of orientalism in that they are both exoticised and demonised. The Rev. Crisparkle is determined to make an English gent/lad out of his charges. However, the narrative quickly differentiates between Helena and Neville. Helena is praised for her self-control and for her courage in protecting Rosa from Jasper's advances as Crisparkle points out to Neville:

> 'Say so; but take this one. Your sister has learnt how to govern what is proud in her nature. She can dominate it even when it is wounded through her sympathy with you. No doubt she has suffered deeply in those same streets where you suffered deeply. No doubt her life is darkened by the cloud that darkens yours. But bending her pride into a grand composure that is not haughty or aggressive, but is a sustained confidence in you and the truth, she has won her way through those streets until she passes along them as high in the general respect as any one who treads them. Every day and hour of her life since Edwin Drood's disappearance, she has faced malignity and folly – for you – as only a brave nature well directed can. So it will be with her to the end. Another and weaker kind of pride might sink broken-hearted, but never such a pride as here: which knows no shrinking, and can get no mastery over her.'
> (Dickens, 1989: 199)

Indeed, Helena is also the only one with any recognised control over her brother's perceived 'vindictive and violent nature' (Dickens, 1989: 184–5). Although the narrative does display sympathy with Neville, he is distrusted and demonised by the community from the onset. He is marked by his violent outbursts and seething resentment, whereas Helena is the one 'that nothing in our misery ever subdued' and who 'showed the daring of a man' (Dickens, 1989: 63). The community generally perceives Neville as 'a dangerously passionate fellow, of an uncontrollable and furious temper'; he is a man to be 'avoided' (Dickens, 1989: 102). Neville's loss of control can be read as the Eastern aspect of his character (his mixed race and his childhood in the colonies). Jasper notes in his diary Neville's 'demoniacal passion', 'his strength in his fury, and his savage rage for the destruction of its object' (Dickens, 1989: 109); all of these qualities allow Jasper to frame Neville for Edwin's murder. Yet perhaps the real paradox in the novel is that the real villain is not Neville but the 'unnaturally dark' Jasper; significantly Jasper is constantly associated with the East and with excess. 'He eats without appetite, and soon goes forth again. Eastward and still eastward through the stale streets he takes his way, until he reaches his destination: a miserable court, espcially miserable among many such' (Dickens, 1989: 263). He displays lack of self-control in his addiction to opium, the use of which establishes him as a degenerate character – something which is reaffirmed in his later actions. Jasper is the 'jaded traveller' whose opium trips are fuelled by an illicit trade of empire. Such contact with empire can be read as degenerative; Jasper is the Englishman gone native, not in the colonies but at the heart of empire. He is prone to violent outbursts and he is rapacious in his dealings with Rosa, Edwin's fiancée.

Ultimately, in *The Mystery of Edwin Drood*, not only have the commodities of empire – Rosa's Lumps-of-Delight, or Sapsea's wine and china cups – made their way back to England but so has the degenerating contagion of empire. So although Jasper is the one who displays the violence and excess associated with the East, because of his family name, social place and blood relations, he possesses a rootedness within the community as a pillar of the church which the Landlesses will never achieve.

Daniel Deronda and *The Mystery of Edwin Drood*, considered together, represent the two pan-European identities of the time: Jews and gypsies. Deronda is Jewish and the Landlesses, through name and complexion, are associated with, among others, the travelling population. In fact, their desire to live a life wandering through England embodies this identity. Both identities then, as Riehl argued at the time, were considered as 'other': 'an internal rootless adversary against whom the host nation could hone its sense of superior identity' (Semmel, 1994: 104–5). However, each narrative offers an ambiguous position for these orphan figures. Deronda embodies the values that Eliot felt that England had lost but should aspire to recover. Yet ultimately there is no place for Deronda in England, and his nation-building project works in conjunction with British imperial aspirations. The Landless twins, however, as products of British colonies, find no welcome in their originary homeland. Or rather, as the twins are simultaneously demonised (Neville) and exoticised (Helena), only certain qualities, namely those embodied by Helena, find a home within England. The inner strength and strength of character which establish Helena as superior/protector to the English rose (Rosa) are singularly lacking in her brother. While, like Eliot, Dickens's narrative is not jingoistic but rather appears to satirise the strident imperialism embodied by Sapsea the ridiculed 'Old Tory Jackass' (Stone, 1987: 383) nevertheless, the narrative, like the society at the time, relies on the assumptions of empire and orientalism in order to locate villainy and allow plot resolution and the re-establishment of good English society. Ultimately, both authors see the 'increasing savagery of English domestic life as a product of the imperial connection' (Perera, 1991: 108).

Epilogue

Jo is brought in. He is not one of Mrs Pardiggle's Tockahoopo Indians; He is not one of Mrs Jellyby's lambs, being wholly unconnected with Borrioboola-Gha; he is not softened by distance and unfamiliarity; he is not a genuine foreign-grown savage; he is the ordinary home-made article. Dirty, ugly, disagreeable to all the senses, in body a common creature of the common streets, only in soul a heathen. Homely filth begrimes him, homely parasites devour him, homely sores are in him, homely rags are on him: native ignorance, the growth of English soil and climate, sinks his immortal nature lower than the beasts that perish. (Dickens, 1892: 513)

THE FIGURE of Jo, the orphan crossing sweep in *Bleak House*, embodies the condition of orphanhood. Illiterate, impoverished, neglected and carrying a plague (smallpox), Jo's existence as 'the growth of English soil and climate' who in soul is a 'heathen' poses problems for notions of the family and national identity. The figure of Jo, afflicted by 'homely grime', 'homely parasites' and 'homely sores', is one who has no knowledge of home ('What's home?' (Dickens, 1892: 119)). His orphanhood is absolute, as is confirmed by the court: 'Name, Jo [no surname] ... No father, no mother, no friends. Never been to school. What's home? Know a broom's a broom, and know it's wicked to tell a lie' (Dickens, 1892: 119). Although Jo insists that he knows 'nothink' what he does know is he is 'scarcely human' (Dickens, 1892: 177): 'He is not of the same order of things, not of the same place in creation. He is of no order and no place; neither of the beasts, nor of humanity' (Dickens, 1892: 513). In his insistence on Jo not being 'a genuine foreign-grown savage' but 'the ordinary home-made article', Dickens is not only making a pointed reference to the philanthropy of Mrs Jellyby – a philanthropy which seeks to help those in foreign climes perhaps because of their exoticism while neglecting the misery and suffering in her own home – but is also establishing the orphan as the difference within, one who is of the nation but simultaneously outside it. This outsider's presence is a dangerous supplement, a subaltern adjunct whose presence disrupts the notions of family, belonging and nation. Jo's physical presence disrupts the two main families in the novel: he carries the plague (smallpox) into the Jarndyce household; and he, if he were but to know it, possesses the key to unlock the secret of Lady Deadlock's former lover and illegitimate daughter.

The larger society, in the form of the constables who police the society, constantly seek to expel Jo – he is continually told to 'move on' but never told where. In fact, society only wants Jo to move on out of sight, to disappear. Jo recognises that the only destination for him is to move on 'to the berryin ground' (Dickens, 1892: 508); his death is what society yearns for; Jo is the scapegoat, the *pharmakos*, whose death is both yearned for and required. Derrida argues that the scapegoat is offered as a ritual sacrifice:

> If a calamity overtook the city ... whether it were famine or pestilence or any other mischief, they led forth as though to a sacrifice the most unsightly of them all as purification and a remedy. ... That representative represents the otherness of the evil that comes to affect or infect the inside by unpredictably breaking into it. Yet the representative of the outside is nonetheless *constituted*, regularly granted its place by the community, chosen, kept, fed, etc., in the very heart of the inside. These parasites were as a matter of course domesticated by the living organism that housed them at its expense. ... When any calamity, such as plague, drought, or famine, befell the city, they sacrificed two of these outcasts as scapegoats.
>
> The ceremony of the *pharmakos* is thus played out on the boundary line between inside and outside .... The origin of difference and division, the pharmakos represents evil both introjected and projected. ... Sacred and accursed. (Derrida, 1981: 133)

Jo embodies the scapegoat, the carrier of the plague, who is paradoxically, as Derrida points out, both sustained (in the sense that he lives) and contained by the family. Yet it is his presence which plagues the family; his presence reveals the family in crisis. The threat Jo poses, i.e., to make visible the secret of the difference contained within the family, necessitates that he be overcome, expelled, sacrificed in order that the family may be seen to regenerate itself.

The orphan functions as a *pharmakon*, a surplus, an excess to be excluded. Conceived of in this way, it is possible then to see how orphanhood became a vehicle for emigration in a scheme which would both rid Britain of its surplus population and settle the colonies with white stock. The emigration schemes highlight the orphan's ambivalent position both at the core of the inside yet on the outside: an insider-out. The orphan is perceived of as a racialised other who is, through emigration, involved in a programme of racial cleansing as Victorian Britain attempted to displace the racialised indigenous other in the colonies. Orphanhood, and the unknown genealogy it implies, is also the embodiment of Victorian culture's fears of illegitimacy and miscegenation; the presence of the orphan unsettles notions of belonging for both family and nation. Yet the orphan figure is continually reproduced by the state, as its presence is necessary for the reaffirmation of ideals of the family and the nation – ideals which were under threat by the expansion of capitalism, industrialisation, the forces of modernity, and empire. As such, the orphan embodies a melancholia, a continual objectification and mourning for the unsustainable ideals of family and nation in Victorian culture.

Appendix

Copy of circular distributed in Canada by Miss Rye

The children vary in age from 9 to 12 years, are all Protestants, and nearly all absolute orphans, are bound (when not adopted) till they are 18 years old, on the following terms, viz., up to 15 years old they are to be fed, clothed, and sent to Sunday school. From 15–17 they are not clothed but paid $3 a month wages, and $4 a month from 17 to 18. If, through any unforeseen circumstances, it is necessary for a child to be returned to the Home, due notice of the same must be given, in writing, a full fortnight before the child is removed; and if the child has been away from the Home six months, her clothes must be returned new and whole, and in same number as they left the Home. In no case may a child be passed on to another family without first consulting Miss Rye, and in case of the death of persons (husband or wife) taking children, it is particularly requested that an immediate notice of the fact be sent to the Home. (PP, 1875, LXIII, 290–1)

Memorandum

Children who have been deserted three years to be considered orphans. If the child in whom you are interested is taken to Canada she will go to 'Our Western Home' Niagara, Canada, West, and will be taken care of until she can be placed out into some respectable farmer's or tradesman's family, and be looked after until she is eighteen years of age. (PP, 1875, LXIII, 291)

Notes

1 However, the paradox in this conception of family is that women are central to this domestic ideal of blood relation and sameness, yet they simultaneously embody the difference within: through marriage women move to a new family. Blood relation, in terms of mother and child, husband and wife, therefore, is a simultaneous relation of sameness and difference. The national ideal of home is therefore more complex than is usually allowed.

2 Girard defines the scapegoat as the victim chosen to embody the ills that are threatening the social body. This sacrificial victim is a 'substitute for all members of the community, offered up by the members themselves ... in whose figure the elements of dissension scattered throughout the community are drawn ... and eliminated ... by its sacrifice' (Girard, 1977: 4–8). The scapegoat is a person, animal or object which is chosen not because of any sense of guilt but because of its marginal social position which makes it lack a crucial social link, establishing it as other. With the destruction of the scapegoat comes the salvation of the community, hence, the scapegoat is not only seen as responsible for the calamity, but through its own destruction responsible for the resultant peace: 'The surrogate victim ... inevitably appears as a being who submits to violence without provoking a reprisal; a supernatural being who sows violence to reap peace; a mysterious saviour who visits affliction on mankind in order subsequently to restore it to good health' (Girard, 1977: 52).

3 Although Thackeray does not make the murder explicit, he has prepared for it by the Clytemnestra scene, the placing of the illustration, the description of Jos's death by the solicitor as the 'blackest case that ever had come before him' (Thackeray, 1985: 796).

4 Froude's melancholic meditation on one removed from home, in exile, homeless and separated from family which ultimately implies being without (or outside the) family, also offers us an interesting analogy between orphanhood and the condition of women on the

Victorian marriage market (both the domestic marriage market and the surplus women market in the colonies). Women as marriageable commodities are then separated from their blood families, and at times communities, through marriage. At best, the women ended up with multiple families (birth family and marriage family). Thus, orphanhood posed women a particular problem in the marriage market; the lack of a known genealogy and the suspicion of illegitimacy that accompanied this lack of genealogy often destroyed the prospects of marriage.

5 For a good discussion of the problematic political implications of Derrida's conceptualisation of the *pharmakon*, read A. Haddour (2000), *Colonial Myths. History and Narrative*, Manchester: Manchester University Press, pp. 196–201.

6 David Miller, *The Novel and the Police*, found in Simon During (1992), *Foucault and Literature: Towards a Genealogy of Writing*, London, Routledge.

7 *cf.*, Edward Said's *Orientalism* (New York: Pantheon, 1978).

8 Take for example the 'blissful' domestic scene at the Linton which Heathcliff and Catherine interrupt. In reality, it is anything but blissful.

'We crept through a broken hedge, groped our way up the path, and planted ourselves on a flower-pot under the drawing room window. The light came from thence; they had not put up the shutters, and the curtains were only half closed. Both of us were able to look in by standing on the basement, and clinging to the ledge, and we saw – ah! it was beautiful – a splendid place carpeted with crimson, and crimson-coverd chairs and tables, and a pure white ceiling bordered by gold, a shower of glass-drops hanging in silver chains from the centre, and shimmering with little soft tapers. Old Mr and Mrs Linton were not there. Edgar and his sister had it entirely to themselves; shouldn't they have been happy? We should have thought ourselves in heaven! And now, guess what your good children were doing? Isabella, I believe she is eleven, a year younger than Cathy, lay screaming at the farther end of the room shrieking as if witches were running red hot needles into her. Edgar stood on the hearth weeping silently, and in the middle of the table sat a little dog shaking its paw and yelping, which, from their mutual accusations, we understood they had nearly pulled in two between them. The idiots! That was their pleasure! ... I'd not exchange, for a thousand lives, my condition here, for Edgar

Linton's at Thrushcross Grange – not if I might have the privilege of flinging Joseph off the highest gable, and painting the house-front with Hindley's blood!' (Bronte, 1968: 53–4).

9 Joseph 'would had he dared, have fostered hate between him and the present owner of the Heights, but his dread of that owner amounted to superstition' (Brontë, 1968: 215).

10 When I refer to *Perils* I will only be considering the sections that Dickens wrote.

11 'You two brave fellows that I had been so grudgeful of, I know that if you were dying you would put it off to get up and do your best, and then you would be so modest that in lying down again to die, you would hardly say, "I did it!"'

'It did me good. It really did me good' (Dickens, 1987; 178).

12 This outfit was very substantial consisting, for each girl of: four frocks; four shifts; six pair of stockings; three pairs of shoes; three flannel petticoats, two upper petticoats; two pair of stays; two bonnets; one woollen shawl; four towels; three pocket-handker-chiefs; one neckerchief; three coloured aprons; a brush; two combs; one lb of soap; needles; thread; worsted; scissors; pens; ink; paper; 2s 6d; a Bible; and a prayer-book. For the boys each had; a canvas jacket, waistcoat and trousers; seven pair of stockings; three pair boots or shoes; five shirts; two neckcloths; three pocket-handker-chiefs; two cloth caps; one south-wester; one lb of soap; two combs; one brush; a large clasp knife; needles; thread; buttons; worsted; darning needles; 2s 6d; a Bible; and prayer-book (PP, 1851, XL, 416). Each child's things were packed in a canvas sack with an inventory.

13 Mr Matthews more than likely found his journey to Canada very different from his journey to Bermuda. Despite the reservations about the legality and motivation behind emigrating these children and the possible life they went to, their passage was, comparatively speaking, well provisioned. One need only compare the descrip-tion of the preparations and provisions provided for the children with that provided for a group of Irish poor who were paying for their passage to emigrate to New York on board the emigrant ship *Washington* in November 1850. The treatment received by these emigrants was so atrocious that Mr Vere Foster, a passenger on board the ship, wrote a letter of complaint to the government. The complaint outlined a brutal regime on board the ship which subjected paying passengers to: brutal assault; not receiving any

provisions (food or water) included in the purchase price for the first four days; receiving barely half the provisions which the ticket price covered; being frequently denied water; adults being declared by ship doctor as children regardless of the fact that they paid the adult fare in order that they, as so-called children, would be then entitled to half the provisions of an adult; the poorest of these passengers being unable to obtain a cooked meal more than once every two days (while those with money to bribe the cook received up to six cooked meals a day); women being forced to share privvies with men; the dead being buried without service. Mr Vere Foster also ascertains that upon arrival he met with passengers who had made earlier voyages on the *Washington* who claimed that on their trip there were no provision issued during the first fortnight and no meat at all. Even more ominously, passengers who had travelled earlier on the *Atlas* claim that their treatment was considerably worse than that received on board the *Washington* (PP, 1851, XL, 434). Allegations of such treatment were serious, especially in light of the fact that during the period 1846–50 1,163,123 emigrated from the UK (England, Scotland, Ireland and Wales) *at their own cost.* This number excludes a number of pauper children emigrated and those whose emigration was assisted (PP, 1851, XL, 444).

14 The missionary nature of the work can be understood as the endeavour to conquer the 'Orient' within by keeping those in the margins of society out. In this case, out meant relegated to the colonies.

15 For a good discussion of the political implications of Derrida's conflation of writing, vagrancy and democracy, cf., A. Haddour, (2000a) 'Citing difference: vagrancy, nomadism and the site of the colonial and postcolonial', in *City Visions*, D. Bell and A. Haddour (eds), Harlow, Addison Wesley Longman, pp. 44–59.

16 Semmel's book offers a full discussion of the issue of inheritance and the conflicting theories of nationalism and cosmopolitanism which influenced Eliot.

17 The notion of like is important because one of the main tenets of cosmopolitanism is that it advocated what we would now view as a liberal humanist point of view in which the notion of difference would be eradicated and all would be united under the rubric of humanity.

18 'The earth was made for Dombey and Son to trade in, and the sun

and moon were made to give them light. Rivers and seas were formed to float their ships; rainbows gave them promise of fair weather; winds blew for or against their enterprises; stars and planets circled in their orbits, to preserve inviolate a system of which they were the centre. Common abbreviations took new meanings in his eyes, and had sole reference to them: A.D. had no concern with anno Domini, but stood for anno Dombei – and Son' (Dickens, 1890: 2).

References

Achebe, C. (1977), 'An image of Africa: racism in Conrad's *Heart of Darkness*', *The Massachusetts Review*, 18: 782–94.

Anon., (1842), *The Orphan's Friend*, London, Religious Tract Society.

Anon., (26 September 1857), 'A very black act', *Household Words*, 293–4.

Anon., (1861a), *Susan Carter, the Orphan Girl*, London, Society for Promoting Christian Knowledge.

Anon., (1861b), *The Workhouse Orphan*, London, Hatchard & Co.

Anon. (1871), 'The orphan sailor boy', *Five Sea Novels*, Glasgow, Cameron and Ferguson.

Auerbach, N. (1975), 'Incarnations of the orphan', *English Literary History*, 42, 395–419.

—— (1985), *Romantic Imprisonment: Women and Other Glorified Outcasts*, New York, Columbia University Press.

—— (1990), *Private Theatricals: The Lives of the Victorians*, Cambridge, Mass., Harvard.

Bhabha, H.K. (1984), 'Of mimicry and men', *October*, 28: 125–33.

Blackford, M. (1840), 'The orphan of Waterloo', *The Holiday Library*, vol. 1, London, Joseph Cundall.

Bowen, C.E. (1881), *Cared For; or the Orphan Wanderers*, London, Partridge & Co.

Brantlinger, P. (1988) *Rule of Darkness: British Literature and Imperialism, 1830–1914*, Ithaca, Cornell University Press.

Bratton, J.S. (1986), 'Of England, home, and duty: the image of England in Victorian and Edwardian fiction', in J.M. Mackenzie (ed.), *Imperialism and Popular Culture*, Manchester, Manchester University Press.

Brontë, C. (1848), *Jane Eyre*, Harmondsworth, Penguin, 1985.

———— (1853), *Villette*, eds Margaret Smith and Herbert Rosengarten, Oxford, Oxford University Press, 1991.

Brontë, E. (1848), *Wuthering Heights*, ed. F.T. Flahiff, Toronto and London, Macmillan, 1968.

Buchan, P. (1834), *The Orphan Sailor: A Tragic Tale of Love, of*

Pity, and of Woe, Edinburgh, Thomas Stevenson.

Burke, E. (1790), *Reflections on the Revolution in France*, ed. T.H.D. Mahoney, Indianapolis, Liberal Arts Press, 1955.

Carlyle, T. (1840), 'On heroes, hero-worship and the heroic in history', *Sartor Resartus* and *On Heroes and Hero Worship*, London, J.M. Dent, 1967.

Carpenter, M. (1968), *Reformatory Schools: For the Children of the Perishing and Dangerous Classes and for Juvenile Offenders*, London, The Woburn Press.

Césaire, A. (1972), *Discourse on Colonialism*, New York, Monthly Review Press.

Collins, P. (1965), *Dickens and Crime*, London, Macmillan.

Collins, W. (1863), *No Name*, Oxford, Oxford University Press, 1992.

Conrad, J. (1899), *Heart of Darkness*, ed. Robert Kimbrough, New York, Norton, 1963.

Cunningham, H. (1991), *The Children of the Poor: Representations of Childhood Since the Seventeenth Century*, Oxford, Blackwell.

Crane, D. (1915), *John Bull's Surplus Children: A Plea for Giving Them a Fairer Chance*, London, Horace Marshall & Son.

Davidoff, L. and Hall, C. (1987), *Family Fortunes: Men and Women of the English Middle Class*, 1780–1850, London, Routledge.

Davin, A. (1996), *Growing Up Poor: Home, School and Street in London 1870–1914*, London, Rivers Oram Press.

Dawson, G. (1994), *Soldier Heroes: British Adventure, Empire and the Imagining of Masculinities*, London, Routledge.

Derrida, J. (1981), *Dissemination*, tr. Barbara Johnson, London, Athlone Press.

—— (1976), *Of Grammatology*, tr. Gayatri Chakravorty Spivak, Baltimore, Johns Hopkins University Press.

Dickens, C. (1838), *The Adventures of Oliver Twist; Or, The Parish Boy's Progress*, ed. Kathleen Tillotson, Oxford, The Clarendon Press, 1966.

—— (1848), *Dombey and Son*, London, Chapman and Hall, 1890.

—— (1848), 'The Haunted Man', *Christmas Books*, Oxford, Oxford University Press, 1987.

—— (1853), *Bleak House*, London, Chapman and Hall, 1892.

—— (1853), 'Frauds on the fairies', *Household Words*, 1 October.

—— (1853), 'The noble savage', *Uncommercial Traveller and Reprinted Pieces*, Oxford, Oxford University Press, 1987.

REFERENCES

—— (1857), *Little Dorrit*, Oxford, Oxford University Press, 1953.

—— (1857), 'The perils of certain English prisoners', *Christmas Books*, Oxford, Oxford University Press, 1987.

—— (1862), *Great Expectations*, Oxford, Oxford University Press, 1987.

—— (1870), *The Mystery of Edwin Drood*, Oxford, Oxford University Press, 1989.

—— (1937–8), *The Letters of Charles Dickens*, 3 vols, ed. Walter Dexter, London, Nonesuch Press.

During, L. (1993), 'The concept of dread: sympathy and ethics in *Daniel Deronda*', *The Critical Review*, 33, 88–111.

Eagleton, T. (1988), *Myths of Power: A Marxist Study of the Brontës*, Basingstoke, Macmillan.

—— (1995), *Heathcliff and the Great Hunger*, London, Verso.

Edmond, R. (1988), *Affairs of the Hearth: Victorian Poetry and Domestic Narrative*, London and New York, Routledge.

Eliot, G. (1856), *The natural history of German life: Riehl, Essays of George Eliot*, (ed.) T. Pinney, New York, Columbia University Press, 1963.

—— (1861), *Silas Marner*, ed. Q.D. Leavis, Harmondsworth, Penguin, 1985.

—— (1876), *Daniel Deronda*, Harmondsworth, Penguin, 1984.

—— (1879), 'The Modern Hep! Hep! Hep!', *The Impressions of Theophrastus Such*, New York, Thomas Nelson, 1925.

Foucault, M. (1979), *The History of Sexuality*, vol. 1., tr. Robert Hurley, London, Allen Lane.

Freud, S. (1915), 'Mourning and melancholia', *On Metapsychology: The Theory of Psychoanalysis*, vol. 11, ed. Albert Dickson, Harmondsworth, Penguin, 1987.

—— (1919), 'The uncanny', *Art and Literature*, vol. 14, Harmondsworth, Penguin, 1987.

Froude, J. (1849), *The Nemesis of Faith*, London and New York, publisher unknown, 1904.

—— (1867–83), *Short Studies on Great Subjects*, 4 vols, London, publisher unknown, 1888.

—— (1872), 'England's war', *Short Studies on Great Subjects*, vol. 2, London, publisher unknown, 1888.

Frye, Northrop (1957), *Anatomy of Criticism*, Princeton, Princeton University Press.

Gilbert, S.M. and Gubar, S. (1979), *The Madwoman in the Attic:*

REFERENCES

The Woman Writer and the Nineteenth-Century Literary Imagination, New Haven, Yale University Press.

Gilmartin, S. (1998), *Ancestry and Narrative in Nineteenth-Century British Literature: Blood Relations from Edgeworth to Hardy*, Cambridge, Cambridge University Press.

Gilead, S. (1987), 'Liminality in Charlotte Brontë's novels', *Texas Studies in Literature and Language*, 29, 302–22.

Girard, R. (1977), *Violence and the Sacred*, tr. Patrick Gregory, London, Johns Hopkins University Press.

Glover, Lizzie (1876), *Victor, The Little Orphan: or, the Necessity of Self-help*, London, Elliot Stock.

Green, M. (1980), *Dreams of Adventure, Deeds of Empire*, London, Routledge & Kegan Paul.

Haddour, A. (2000), 'Citing difference: vagrancy, nomadism and the site of the colonial and postcolonial', in D. Bell and A. Haddour (eds), *City Visions*, Harlow, Addison Wesley Longman, 44–59.

—— (2000a), *Colonial Myths: History and Narrative*, Manchester, Manchester University Press.

Hassam, A. (1994), *Sailing to Australia: Shipboard Diaries by Nineteenth-Century British Emigrants*, Manchester, Manchester University Press.

Houghton, W. (1957), *The Victorian Frame of Mind, 1830–1870*, New Haven and London, Yale University Press.

Howe, I. (1979), 'George Eliot and the Jews', *Partisan Review*, XLVI, 359–75.

Hughes, R. (1987), *The Fatal Shore*, London, Pan.

Hutchins, F.G. (1967), *The Illusion of Permanence: British Imperialism in India*, Princeton, Princeton University Press.

Innes, C.L. (1990), *The Devil's Own Mirror: The Irishman and the African in Modern Literature*, Washington, Three Continents Press, Inc.

James, L. (1974), *Fiction for the Working Man*, Harmondsworth, Penguin.

—— (1978), *Print and the People 1819–1851*, Harmondsworth, Penguin.

Kristeva, J. (1991), *Strangers to Ourselves*, tr. Leon S. Roudiez, London, Harvester Wheatsheaf.

Leavis, F.R. (1949), *The Great Tradition: George Eliot, Henry James, Joseph Conrad*, New York, George W. Stewart.

REFERENCES

Lesjak, C. (1996), 'Labours of a modern storyteller: George Eliot and the cultural project of "Nationhood" in Daniel Deronda', in Ruth Robbins and Julian Wolfreys (eds), *Victorian Identities: Social and Cultural Formations in Nineteenth-Century Literature*, Basingstoke, Macmillan.

Linehan, K. Bailey. (1992), Mixed politics: the critique of imperialism, *Daniel Deronda, Texas Studies in Literature and Language*, 34: 3, 323–46.

Macaulay, R. (1924), *Orphan Island*, London, Collins.

Mackenzie, J. (ed.) (1986), *Imperialism and Popular Culture*, Manchester, Manchester University Press.

Marx, K. and Engels, F. (1848), *The Communist Manifesto*, Harmondsworth, Penguin, 1967.

Matthews, E. (1863), *The Orphan Boy: on How Little John was Reclaimed*, London, George Watson.

Memmi, A. (1957), *The Colonizer and the Colonized*, London, Souvenir Press, 1974.

Meyer, S. (1993), '"Safely to their own borders": proto-Zionism, feminism, and nationalism', *English Literary History*, 60, 773–58.

—— (1996), *Imperialism at Home: Race and Victorian Women's Fiction*, Ithaca, Cornell University Press.

Moore, W.J. (1862), *Health in the Tropics: or, Sanitary Art Applied to Europeans in India*, London, Churchill.

Mootoo (pseud.) (1850), *The Orphan; A Romance*, London, Arthur Hall, Virtue & Co.

Nandy, A. (1983), *The Intimate Enemy: Loss and Recovery of Self Under Colonialism*, New Delhi, Oxford University Press.

Newman, J. H. (1967), *Apologia Pro Vita Sua: Being a History of His Religious Opinions*, ed. Martin J. Sraglic, London, Clarendon Press.

O'Toole, T. (1997), *Genealogy and Fiction in Hardy: Family Lineage and Narrative Lines*, Basingstoke, Macmillan.

Parliamentary Papers – these are noted by year, volume and page number in the text denoted by PP.

Perera, S. (1991), *Reaches of Empire: The English Novel from Edgeworth to Dickens*, New York, Columbia University Press.

Peters, L. (2000), 'Double-dyed traitors and villains: *The Illustrated London News*, Charles Dickens, *Household Words* and the Indian Mutiny' in D. Finkelstein and M. Peers (eds), *Negotiating India in Nineteenth-Century Media*, London, Macmillan.

REFERENCES

Plasa, C. and Ring, B. (1994), *The Discourse of Slavery: Aphra Behn to Toni Morrison*, London, Routledge.

Ruskin, J. (1902–12) *Works*, eds E. Cook and A. Wedderburn, vol. 18, London, publisher unknown.

Said, E. (1978), *Orientalism*, New York, Pantheon.

—— (1979), 'Zionism from the standpoint of its victims', *Social Text*, 1: 17–22.

Semmel, B. (1994), *George Eliot and The Politics of National Inheritance*, Oxford, Oxford University Press.

Smith, L. (1842), *Abiah, Or, The Record of a Foundling*, London, publisher unknown.

Steedman, C. (1988), *The Radical Soldier's Tale: John Pearman, 1819–1908*, London, Routledge.

—— (1990), *Childhood, Culture and Class in Britain: Margaret McMillan 1860–1931*, London, Virago.

Stone, H. (1987), *Dickens's Working Notes for His Novels*, Chicago, Chicago University Press.

Tambling, J. (1995), *Dickens, Violence and the Modern State: Dreams of the Scaffold*, London, Macmillan.

Thackeray, W.M. (1848), *Vanity Fair*, Harmondsworth, Penguin, 1985.

Thomson, A. (1856), *Punishment and Prevention*, found in Anon. *The Workhouse Orphan* (1816b), London, Hatchard & Co.

Vicinus, M. (1974), *The Industrial Muse: A Study of Nineteenth-Century British Working-Class Literature*, London, Croom Helm.

Walkowitz, J.R. (1980), *Prostitution and Victorian Society: Women, Class and the State*, Cambridge, Cambridge University Press.

Wall, C. (1838), *The Orphan's Isle; a Tale for Youth, Founded on Facts*, London, W.S. Orr.

Wilde, O. (1891), *The Picture of Dorian Gray*, Harmondsworth, Penguin Books, 1949.

Wood, Mrs H. (1861), *East Lynne*, Stroud, Alan Sutton, 1993.

Young, R. (1995), *Colonial Desire: Hybridity in Theory, Culture and Race*, London, Routledge.

Index

Note: literary works can be found under authors' names, 'n.' after a page reference indicates the number of a note on that page.

156